Camping the North Shore

Explore the Shore!

Andrew Vale

Other titles in the series:

Skiing the North Shore: A guide to cross country trails in Minnesota's spectacular Lake Superior region

Camping the North Shore

A guide to the 23 best campgrounds
in Minnesota's spectacular Lake Superior region

ANDREW SLADE

THERE AND
BACK BOOKS
READ. GO. DISCOVER.

Duluth, Minnesota

Camping the North Shore
A guide to the 23 best campgrounds in Minnesota's
spectacular Lake Superior region

Cover and book design: Sally Rauschenfels
Editing and proofreading: Gail Trowbridge

Photography credits: All photographs © Andrew Slade unless otherwise noted. Cover © Jeffrey Smith; back cover (top) © Lanica Klein, (bottom) © istockphoto Inc.; p. 24 © Alan Heartfield; p. 28 © Michael Westhoff; p. 50 © Megasquib|Dreamstime.com; p. 55 © Michael Thompson; p. 69 © Ben Blankenburg; p. 89 & 91 © Dennis O'Hara; p. 92 © Carl Foster; p. 93 © Dan Thornberg; p. 109 © Travis Novitsky; p. 114 (top) © Elizabeth Lilja

ISBN 978-0-9794675-1-6

Library of Congress Control Number: 2007910279

Printed in Canada by Friesens
First printing, March 2008

There & Back Books
1026 S. Lake Ave., Duluth, Minnesota 55802 Tel (218) 727-4873
www.thereandbackbooks.com

THERE AND
BACK BOOKS
READ. GO. DISCOVER.

*To Sally, whom I've loved ever since
that first camping trip, and
To our son Noah, who really knows how to
pick a great campsite.*

Table of Contents

Camping the North Shore: The 23 best campgrounds

Minnesota

Isabella ⓞ ➏

Silver Bay ⚬

➌

Lake
Superior

Two Harbors ⚬

⚬ Duluth
⚬ Superior

➊

➊ Jay Cooke State Park
➋ Burlington Bay
➌ Indian Lake
➍ Gooseberry Falls State Park
➎ Split Rock Lighthouse State Park
➏ Eighteen Lake
➐ Eckbeck
➑ Finland
➒ Ninemile Lake
➓ Tettegouche State Park
⑪ Lamb's Resort
⑫ Temperance River State Park

⑬ Temperance River Nat'l. Forest
⑭ Sawbill Lake
⑮ Baker Lake
⑯ Crescent Lake
⑰ Cascade River State Park
⑱ Grand Marais RV Park
   and Campground
⑲ Devil Track
⑳ Two Island
㉑ Kimball Lake
㉒ Trail's End
㉓ Judge C.R. Magney State Park

Tofte

Grand Marais

Foreword

IT WAS JUST AFTER MIDNIGHT when we were awakened by the snap of breaking branches. Something big was moving our way. We sat up in our sleeping bags and listened as it slowly came closer. It was only feet from the tent when we decided to get a glimpse of our uninvited guest, but the noise from opening the tent zipper spooked it toward the lake. That's when we heard splashing and realized we'd had a very close encounter with a moose. It took a while before we could drift back to sleep.

That is only one of thousands of memories we have made while camping along Minnesota's North Shore. Waking up to the call of a loon, sitting around the campfire watching for the first stars to appear, or taking in the magic of the full moon rising over Lake Superior—all of these are experiences that, as a family, we will never forget.

As manager of Gooseberry Falls State Park I have the privilege of helping others enjoy the same things that our family loves. Seeing the excitement in a child's eyes when they are camping for the first time is quite a thrill. Camping is one of the best ways to bring families closer and make memories that will be cherished for a lifetime.

We can be thankful to all the visionaries who set aside so much public land on the North Shore for all of us to enjoy. But camping on the North Shore has changed over the years. In the past it was easy to find an empty campsite, but more and more visitors have discovered the North Shore. Today, reservations go fast and campgrounds fill up quickly. Planning ahead is an essential part of making your North Shore camping trip a memory maker.

This book can help with those preparations. It gives you the necessary information to plan your trip, including descriptions of over 1000 North Shore area campsites. As you experience this beautiful part of the world, remember to do your part to preserve these places for the generations to come.

— *Paul Sundberg, Photographer & Park Ranger,*
Gooseberry Falls State Park

Acknowledgements

THERE MUST BE SOMETHING SPECIAL about camping on the North Shore. So many people helped pull this guide together, and their enthusiasm for the North Shore and camping was inspirational. Gary Hoeft of Tettegouche State Park was not only the original inspiration, but also a vital source of information as we progressed. It turns out that Tettegouche also manages two other state parks and two state forest campgrounds, so Gary is practically the king of the camping world.

Dan Roth and Lisa Angelos at Split Rock Lighthouse State Park helped explain the intricacies of their system. Jaxan Goodsky sat with me at the picnic area of Temperance River State Park and shared his experience and vision of that gem of a park. Ty Gangelhoff and Richard Hoskins helped me understand the issues at Cascade River State Park.

Steve Schug of the Superior National Forest was very patient with a whole series of e-mail questions about National Forest campgrounds. Ellen Hawkins of the National Forest helped me understand how Leave No Trace ethics apply to car camping and not just to the deep wilderness.

Skip and Linda Lamb shared their pride in their landmark family resort in Schroeder.

Friendly people behind the desk at Burlington Bay and Grand Marais municipal campgrounds were kind to me as I poked around their facilities and asked unusual questions.

Dorian Grilley and Judy Erickson of the Parks and Trails Council of Minnesota fired up my civic side and got me advocating for these parks and campgrounds in the community and in the Legislature. If you love our state parks, this is a great organization to join.

I am appreciative of Gordon and Gerri Slabaugh and all the folks at Adventure Publications for their understanding of how our books reach and help recreational users in the region.

My wife, Sally Rauschenfels, and our two boys, Hans and Noah, are the people I most want to read this book. I want to camp with them, at any of these campgrounds. I can see them there. Noah can pick out the perfect campsite from 100 yards away. Hans is the Field General of Play, and will discover every hiding hole and reading perch within minutes of arrival. For almost 20 years, Sally has been my camping buddy, and now my publishing partner. As in the song "Wild Thing," she makes my heart sing…she makes everything groovy.

Preface

CAMPGROUNDS ARE PLACES OF MAGIC. Overnight, they transform a random collection of strangers into a neighborhood. They turn parents and kids into a family again. Camping restores our deep connections to nature. A campfire connects us with our Paleolithic ancestors in ways a PBS video never could.

I wrote this book so others could experience the magic as I have. I want families to send their kids spinning around the campground on their bikes again. I want evening ranger programs. I want people up at midnight, out in the wind and thunder, to stake out the tent because a thunderstorm is rolling through. This book is not just about where to camp, but also about what to do when you're there.

We need camping on the North Shore now more than ever. The family's traditional week at the Temperance River campground has been replaced by a long weekend, if that. Ghost stories around the campfire have been replaced by satellite TV at the motel.

In an age of affluence, why camp when you can afford to stay in a resort? Because it's good for you. Because the adventure starts the moment you wake up, not after the breakfast bar and morning shower. Because your kids will learn how badly you snore. Because you'll be tested by conditions that are both safe and far out of the ordinary. Lifelong memories start when you're camping. You'll always remember the bear in your campsite, but not the "Law and Order" reruns in the hotel room.

I've always been a tent camper. I spent a year of college traveling around the country with the Audubon Expedition Institute, camping every night in national parks, national forests, on the edge of Indian reservations and off in the wilderness. I've been a wilderness guide in the BWCA, Quetico, and the Rocky Mountains. Sally and I fell in love on a car camping trip to Montana. My family's fondest memories are of camping and hiking in the desert canyon country of Utah.

Although I've always been a tent camper, this book is for all campers—people in tents, in RVs, in pop-up trailers. To be honest, there have been a lot of cold long nights in the tent when we really wanted the heat and light of an RV. Those pop-up trailer beds are looking pretty cozy to our aging backs. The natural resources of the North Shore area are big enough for everyone, regardless of their rig.

A guide to the campsite of your dreams

FOR A GREAT VACATION, camping on Minnesota's spectacular North Shore is an excellent choice. Camping is the best way to experience natural areas, and the North Shore has some of the best parks, forests and trails in the entire Midwest.

Lake Superior is one of our world's wonders. It's the largest freshwater lake on the surface of the world. And it's stunningly beautiful. The lake sits in a massive geologic bowl carved out of some of the oldest rocks in the world.

The Minnesota shoreline of Lake Superior is known as the North Shore. For geologic, historic and geographic reasons, it's both the most rugged shoreline on Lake Superior and the most developed shoreline as well.

Lucky us. To enjoy the scenery and experience the habitats here, we just drive in. If we were camping on the Ontario shore of Lake Superior, we would have to paddle sea kayaks 50 miles along the shore for terrain like this. On the Michigan shore, we might have to beat our way through 50 miles of gravel roads for campgrounds like these. For car campers, the North Shore is paradise.

But this paradise requires planning. If you want to camp on the shore of the lake, you have to plan far ahead. It used to be that all the campsites, even the "best" ones, were available on a first-come, first-served basis. Since 2005, you must reserve a specific campsite months in advance for virtually every shoreline campground.

There's more to the North Shore than those seven state parks and three municipal or private campgrounds right on the water's edge. The North Shore experience goes far inland, and so do the campgrounds. If you're willing to drive a little bit farther and if you can follow a good road map, you can find a good campsite any day.

What's the best campground for you? First, you'll need to make a few choices to find the campsite of your dreams.

Inland or lakeshore

This book describes about 600 sites in campgrounds right on the shore, and about 400 sites that are up to a one-hour drive inland. Sure there are great campsites at Split Rock or Tettegouche, right on the lakeshore. But the most quiet and most remote campgrounds are away from the lake, on beautiful little lakes or along rushing rivers.

Why go inland to camp? In early summer, it will be warmer away from the big chill of Lake Superior water. If you like to fish, the fishing is better. If you like to canoe, you'll find the canoeing is better. If you like loons, you'll see and hear more of them away from the big lake. If you have no reservation, you can find a campsite inland.

Why stay on the shore to camp? The hiking is better. The campgrounds are more convenient, closer to towns and on paved roads. You can reserve a campsite, making that first day a bit less stressful. The views can be spectacular. Depending on the wind direction, the bugs might be better here…or worse.

National forest or state park

Twenty of our top 23 campgrounds are on state or federal public land.

State park campgrounds are the deluxe version of public land camping. All the North Shore state park campgrounds have site-specific reservations, hot showers and flush toilets. There are water faucets throughout the campground. State parks also have the best recreational opportunities, with trail systems leading right from the campground. State park campgrounds are generally RV-friendly; a few even have electric hook-ups and dump stations. They are full almost every night in the summer. If you camp in a state park, you will have to purchase a day or season vehicle permit for the park as well as pay your camping fee.

Superior National Forest campgrounds are a bit more rugged. Most are first-come, first-served. Most are on a nice quiet inland lake. This book lists two types: "Fee Campgrounds" and "Rustic Campgrounds."

Superior National Forest "Fee Campgrounds" have all the basic facilities: running water (generally from one solar-powered pump), vault toilets, and garbage service. The cost to camp is about one-third less than the state parks. The only campground with site reservations detailed in this book is Trail's End. The rest are first-come, first-served. Many have a campground host. Many are managed by private concessionaires, which explains why your check might be written to "Skidder Lady" instead of "Superior National Forest."

Superior National Forest "Rustic Campgrounds" are a real treat. These are small campgrounds, generally just three to five sites. The sites are designed for tents, so you might have to squeeze to get RVs and tent trailers in. There will be one vault toilet. Each site has a picnic table and a fire ring, but there are no other services, meaning no drinking water and no garbage pick-up. You should pack out everything you pack in. These sites, often on pretty little lakes, are free. Spend a night at one of these and you've covered the cost of this book. Although rustic sites have no water supply, they are all on lakes or rivers, where you can draw water for washing. With filtration or boiling, you can drink lake water too.

State forest campgrounds fall somewhere in between state park and national forest campgrounds in terms of services. This book details three: Indian Lake, Eckbeck, and Finland. State forest campgrounds have drinking water, either from a hand pump or from an artesian well. They have vault toilets and garbage service. These campgrounds are managed by nearby state parks. You can't reserve an individual site, although group sites can be reserved.

Private or public.

This book goes into detail on only one private campground—Lamb's Resort in Schroeder. There used to be a lot more private campgrounds on the North Shore, but they're disappearing fast. As this book was being researched, three lakeshore private campgrounds went out of business. Private land, especially the scenic kind where there's a campground, tends to get purchased and turned into condos.

This really makes us all appreciate public lands so much more. We all own it and we're not selling. The land is managed for us by caring professionals.

Ten of our top 23 campgrounds are in the Superior National Forest. Eight of them are in Minnesota state parks. Every morning, when you wake up in these places, pause a moment to thank the visionaries who helped to set aside this land.

RV park or a tenter's paradise

Some of the campgrounds in this book, like Burlington Bay in Two Harbors, are really only meant for RV campers. Tenters will feel out of place there. Other tent-friendly campgrounds, including Temperance River State Park, Jay Cooke State Park, and Trail's End, have electric or water hook-ups available.

However, most of the campgrounds in this book are used by all types of campers. Adventurous RV campers can go way out in the boonies to camp. To do so, RV campers will need to be self-sufficient and plan ahead for fresh water and dump stations. If you're running a generator, respect the desire of your neighbors for quiet. If you need a pull-through site, there are few away from the RV parks.

Nowadays, a pop-up trailer is almost indistinguishable from some of the big family tents. If you have a pop-up trailer or can borrow one, you'll find great camping anywhere described in this book.

You know what you like. You know what your ideal campsite looks like. And you'll find it on the North Shore.

Spring, summer, fall...or winter

Spring comes late to the North Shore, and so do the campers. Even after a long winter, the snow may not be all melted near the shore by May 1. There can be snow inland from the lake until mid-May.

Most campgrounds start to open up in mid-May. The water gets turned back on, the vault toilets get their toilet paper restocked. On Memorial Day weekend many popular campgrounds will be full. Then from late May to early June, there is a bit of a lull.

From mid-June to Labor Day is by far the busiest time for North Shore campgrounds. Near the shoreline itself, most campsites are full every night. Farther inland, all the "primo" campsites are taken almost every night. Families on summer vacation are the main campers now. It is also peak time for insects. August might be the perfect month for family camping, with fewer insects and smaller crowds.

Fall is probably the nicest time to camp on the North Shore, especially the month of September. The insects are gone, the crowds are gone, but there's still all the hiking, biking, paddling or fishing you'd like in the summer. Grouse hunters use inland campgrounds for the season that starts mid-September. The last weekend in September and the first weekend in October are peak fall color times, and most of the popular campgrounds will be full.

By October 1, temperatures start to drop below freezing, so tent campers have to be prepared for cool nights, with the right sleeping bags and pads. Through October, RV campers with heaters make up most of the campers.

Most campgrounds shut down when the real freeze kicks in. The managers shut down the water systems, then stop emptying the garbage and cleaning the outhouses. But if you have a good warm tent or a self-sufficient RV, you can easily continue camping until the snow flies.

In winter, when the snow is on the ground, most of these campgrounds are officially closed. The campground roads generally aren't plowed. State parks do maintain some facilities for winter campers. For example, while the shower houses are closed for the season, every state park campground also has vault toilets. At Cascade River State Park, a warming house right in the campground can be used for your meals and for staying out of the cold until bedtime. At Jay Cooke State Park, reserve the camping cabin and enjoy its rustic heat; flush toilets are available at the River Inn.

Winter tent camping is an art onto itself. Dog mushers have figured out a great system for camping with a canvas wall tent and a collapsible metal stove for burning wood. Car campers can do this too; your car can haul more gear than dogs can. For more information, read *Snow Walker's Companion: Winter Camping Skills for the North*, by Garrett Conover and Alexandra Conover.

Camping on the North Shore is a great choice for a vacation or an adventure. Seek out new wild places and enjoy these rocks, woods and waters!

LIGHT YOUR FIRE...BUT SAVE THE TREES

For many, an evening campfire is as important to camping as the tent. But firewood has lately been a source of real ecological danger on the North Shore. Do your part to help protect these forests from insect infestations.

Firewood can carry forest pests into new areas. The main pest of concern on the North Shore is the Emerald Ash Borer, which can destroy ash forests. The Emerald Ash Borer has been slowly spreading out of the Ohio area and has killed millions of trees.

Don't bring firewood from home. The Minnesota DNR strongly recommends that you purchase firewood from local vendors instead of bringing your own. While the DNR recommends using local firewood, the Superior National Forest takes it a step further, prohibiting firewood from outside Minnesota.

Want to gather your own wood? Be aware that gathering your own firewood from the forest is not allowed in Minnesota state parks. In Superior National Forest and state forest campgrounds, go ahead and gather your own. However, you can use only trees that are already dead and down.

For more information: www.emeraldashborer.info

Insects: dare and prepare

CAMPING ON THE NORTH SHORE often involves close encounters with insects, unless you happen to be out in late fall or very early spring. To be honest, when the insects are bad, it can ruin your day. And there is no way to predict exactly when the insects will be bad. The best thing you can do is prepare.

Ticks. If you're camping early in the season, watch out for ticks. The regular American Dog Tick is a pest on its own, but the Deer Tick has changed everything, with its threat of Lyme disease. As of 2001, there had been no reported cases of Lyme disease in Lake or Cook counties. But ticks are still no fun. The Minnesota DNR recommends using a tick repellent that contains permethrin on clothing. Also, keep your pants tucked into your socks.

Black flies. Black flies lead off the flying insect calendar. Local author and naturalist Larry Weber writes affectionately, "the swarms begin feeding in late May." Black flies are teeny little bloodsuckers that for some reason love the skin under your ears. As with the mosquito, it's only the females that bite us, to help them lay eggs. Black flies hatch from swift-flowing streams, so anywhere there's a gurgling river or stream nearby, there are likely to be black flies. Black flies are out all day long. Their ability to drive woodsmen crazy is legendary. One good thing about black flies: it's said they pollinate blueberry flowers.

University of Minnesota Extension recommends that you "avoid areas with high black fly populations, such as lowlands, areas with dense vegetation or sheltered and shady areas." That sounds like a lot of campgrounds. They also say to "avoid times when black flies are most active, generally at dawn, and dusk." Of course, that's when you're at your campsite the most.

Minnesota Extension has this advice that's useful for campers:

• Wear white or brightly colored clothing. Dark blue shirts are particularly attractive to black flies.

• Cover up bare skin with shoes, socks, long sleeve shirts, long pants, and hats.

• Don't rely on insect repellents, such as those with DEET, although they may provide some relief.

Mosquitoes. Mosquitoes arrive shortly after the black flies. By mid-June, mosquitoes are out almost every evening. During the day, the mosquitoes will be thick in the deep woods, out of the wind. But as the sun goes down, they come out for dinner everywhere. It seems like different strains of mosquitoes come out all summer —there are the little, quick ones, the big, slow and lazy ones. There are about 50 mosquito species in Minnesota, and 28 of those bite humans.

The worst thing about mosquitoes is that they come out in force at night. Just as the sun is going down and you're gathering around the campfire for s'mores and ghost stories, they begin to bite. Fortunately, insect repellents work well on mosquitoes; the kid-friendly DEET blends are often chosen over the 100% DEET that melts your nylon jacket. Long pants and baggy shirts help keep the bites away. Choosing a campsite on a point of land that catches a good breeze is another way to beat them. And a head net can make campsite chores much more pleasant when mosquitoes are active.

Flies and other favorites. Directly along the Lake Superior shoreline, the mosquitoes aren't the worst of the insects—perhaps the lake winds drive them away. Down by Lake Superior, you'll find the stable flies. Stable flies look like ordinary house flies, but they are biters, and the bites hurt. If you're sitting, they go right for your ankles. When there is a strong northwest wind (blowing off the land toward the lake), the stable flies can be awful.

Other local "favorites" are the big, slow horse flies and the pesky, smaller deer flies. They are out during the day but are not active at night. Horse fly bites really hurt, but the flies themselves are easy to swat. Deer flies crawl into your hair. When they bite, the bite site tends to bleed.

Finally, there are two or three nights every summer, warm and humid nights with no wind, when the no-see-ums are out. These tiny midges can get into most older tents just by squeezing through the screens. If you're buying a new tent, make sure it has no-see-um netting.

For your North Shore camping trip, a screen tent for your kitchen area is highly recommended. During the day, when you're off hiking or boating or sightseeing, the insects won't be a problem. But in the afternoon and evenings, back at the campsite, you'll want the protection a screen tent can provide. Good screen tents will set up right over your campsite picnic table, leaving the ground bare. In your screen tent, you can cook your meals on a stove, eat your dinner, and read books all day long. Just don't pitch it over your campfire!

A good ten-foot by ten-foot screen tent might cost $200, but it could save your vacation.

No one really likes these insects. But try to remember that they are part of the wild nature you've come to experience. If you're prepared mentally and physically, you can still have a great camping experience despite their greedy, grubby ways. Be prepared with the right gear, clothing and attitude and you'll have a great time.

Things to bring

ANY GOOD REGULAR CAMPER already has a checklist of things to pack. Yet camping the North Shore is a bit different than camping other places. This isn't a complete equipment list, but these things are particularly useful for North Shore camping:

Toilet paper. You never know when the campground outhouse might run out of TP. Your own supply can be especially important at remote campgrounds and Superior National Forest "Rustic" campgrounds.

Big water jugs. It's a long way from the water tap to your campsite, so one sturdy five-gallon jug will save you some trips. If there is no water at your campground, fill a few five-gallon jugs at home and bring them along. The rigid plastic jugs with a pour spout work great.

A good map. The Superior National Forest's big two-sided map is your best tool for finding out-of-the-way campgrounds. Seventeen of the 23 campgrounds detailed in this book are on this map. Pick it up at any Forest Service office or at many North Shore convenience stores. Gazetteers, such as the DeLorme or Sportsman's Connection, are good as well.

Water filter. If you're staying at a rustic campground, you can use the water right out of the lake or river. You just have to treat it for drinking. Water filters come in all sizes. Try one of the family-sized drip-style water filters, so you always have drinking water "on tap."

Canoe or kayak. Almost all North Shore campgrounds have a lake or river right next to them. If you have a canoe or kayak, bring it with you. Little 10- or 12-foot one-person kayaks are great for spinning around small lakes. Or you can fit a family of four into most canoes.

Screen tent. Insects can be awful. A good screen tent can save your vacation. You can hang out in the screen tent at your site's picnic table from dusk to bedtime, or anytime during the day that the insects get bad.

Swimsuits. Few of these campgrounds have a designated swimming area. But on a hot July day, there's always somewhere to get wet. Even Lake Superior's cold water is tempting in the summer heat. Swimsuits keep you modest and dry off quicker than your cutoff blue jeans.

Fishing pole. Even if you're not a seasoned angler yourself, give it a try. Don't forget the license.

Checkbook and pen. Campers self-register at National Forest and State Forest campgrounds. Those metal boxes don't take credit cards, and you might not have the exact bills with you.

Warm hat and gloves. You never know how cold it might get, especially right by Lake Superior. Dig into your winter gear and bring some fleece or wool for your head and hands.

State park permit. Some of the best and wildest parts of our state parks are only reached from trailheads and picnic areas inside the park. These require a state park permit, either daily or annual. Even if you're not camping at a state park, you'll want to visit them and see their best parts.

A note on cell phones: cellular phone coverage on the North Shore is pretty spotty, especially inland. (That's a good thing when you're on vacation, right?) If you absolutely must be in touch with the office, stick closer to the shoreline and close to towns like Two Harbors or Grand Marais.

Jay Cooke State Park Carlton, Minnesota

A can't-miss feature of Jay Cooke State Park is a trip across the swinging bridge, where kids love to make the bridge creak, and adults watch the St. Louis River rage below. You'll find great scrambling on ancient slate along the river's edge, as well as hiking trails galore.

JAY COOKE STATE PARK has a great family campground, with a wide range of activities and easy camping. Like most state park campgrounds, this one is well maintained and features facilities such as flush toilets and hot showers. Unlike most state park campgrounds on the North Shore, Jay Cooke also has RV sites with electrical hook-ups.

The campground is made up of four loops, each with a distinct character. The first loop, with sites #4-23, is the most rustic of the loops. Sites #10 and 11 back up to big pines and a nice outcrop of slate. A connector trail to the park's "CCC Trail" is right off of sites

#11, 12 and 13. The second loop, sites #24-37, has only nonreservable sites, with site #33 being the nicest.

The middle loops, sites #38-47 and sites #48-64, are the most civilized of all, mostly set up for RVs and proximity to the bathrooms.

The far right loop, sites #65-80, are more wooded and private. The three walk-in sites are private and pleasant but not spectacular.

The campground features the first-ever state park "camper cabin" in northeastern Minnesota, allowing a family without a tent an opportunity to enjoy the state park camping experience. This one features a double bed and three single beds, and a screen porch. There are electric lights but no kitchen, so all cooking goes on outdoors. The cabin can be reserved up to a year in advance through www.stayatmnparks.com.

From the campground, it's a short stroll to the Swinging Bridge area, with the park visitor center and the famous bridge over the St. Louis River. Hiking trails go in every direction, including some starting right in the campground. Bring your bikes; there's a direct connection to the Willard Munger bike trail. Mountain bikers can explore 13 miles of trails in the park.

OPERATED BY
Minnesota State Parks

OPEN
Year-round, but limited facilities October–May.

SITES
83, including 20 electric, a camper cabin, and 4 walk-in sites, plus two group sites. Vehicle length limit 60 ft.

GETTING A SITE
54 sites are reservable. 29 are first-come, first-served. Check at park office across the road.

RESERVATIONS
Visit www.stayatmnparks.com or call (866) 85PARKS.

FACILITIES
Flush and vault toilets, drinking water, showers, dump station.

FEES
$18, $22 for sites with electricity, plus state park permit.

CONTACT
Jay Cooke State Park
780 Highway 210
Carlton, Minnesota 55718
(218) 384-4610
www.dnr.state.mn.us/state_parks/jay_cooke

You'll enjoy these activities & features

★ Fishing: trout
★ Hiking trails
★ State park interpretive programs & nature store
★ Handicapped accessible sites

Jay Cooke
State Park
Campground

to CCC Trail

to CCC Trail

N

Sites #65-80

Sites #48-64

Sites #24-37

Sites #4-23

Walk-in #81-83

Group #2

P

to River Inn

Group #1

Sites #38-47

to River Inn

to Carlton & I-35

210

to Duluth

to Park Office

GETTING THERE

Take Highway 210 east from I-35 and go through the town of Carlton another 3 miles. From Duluth, take Highway 23 (Grand Avenue) south to Fond du Lac, then turn right at Highway 210.

Site #11 (left) backs right up to rocks and a hiking trail. The St. Louis River (right) rushes through the park.

Explore the swinging bridge area

Just across the road from the campground is the hub of the park's activities. In the main park building, called the **River Inn**, you'll find a nice little natural history museum, a beautiful old dark stone and wood great room, and the typical information desk and bookstore. This is actually one of the largest structures built in the state park system, and once included a restaurant. But the real treat is the St. Louis River and the swinging bridge that crosses it. The 200-ft. bridge was built by the CCC in 1934. You'll hear it before you see it, since it creaks loudly with every footstep. The view of the river is tremendous, with hundreds of rivulets pouring in from every direction. On the far side of the bridge, dramatic barren rock invites exploration.

Hike all day

Stop at the information desk and find out more about the 50 miles of hiking trails in the park. There's sure to be one just right for you. From the campground, you can cross the swinging bridge and circle through the maple forest of the Ridge trails. The Silver Creek trail makes for a nice 3.3 mile loop. Right out of the campground, you can take the level **CCC Trail** west to the **Thomson Trail** and visit the historic Thomson pioneer cemetery. You could even hike the **Grand Portage Trail** and ponder the life of the voyageur, or do the very first section of the Superior Hiking Trail.

Ride the Munger Trail

Did you bring your bikes? Right out of the campground road, the Forbay Trail is a paved bike trail that links up with the **Willard Munger State Trail**. The Forbay Trail is hilly and curvy, but the Munger Trail is flat and straight. You can ride the Munger Trail all the way to Duluth, or the other way to Hinckley. For a short, flat ride with kids, go left (or west) about three miles to the Thomson Bridge. For a longer, hillier ride, go right (or east) about seven miles to the scenic Elys Peak area. Download a map of the trail from www.dnr.state.mn.us/state_trails/maps.html.

Burlington Bay Two Harbors, Minnesota

Down on the shores of Burlington Bay, it's hard to believe you're right in town and in an RV park. These stairs lead directly from the campground. Built for RV campers, this campground has a few spots for tenters, too.

THIS CAMPGROUND IS ALL ABOUT LOCATION. Perched over a cobblestone beach with great views of Burlington Bay, and right on the edge of charming Two Harbors, it's a great destination for RV campers. Like its bigger sister up the shore, the Grand Marais RV Park and Campground, this one is right on the lakeshore and right on the edge of town. There are a lot of spaces for RVs of all sizes, though some campers will feel squeezed in because the sites are close together. There are convenience stores, a Dairy Queen and a golf course within a few blocks.

Tent campers may feel a little out of place here. There are sites near the entrance and between the main sections that are better for tent camping, with trees and a bit of privacy. These so-called "primitive" sites have no hook-ups. They are labelled with letters instead of numbers. F, G and H are the nicest of these. RV sites #14-18 also make for decent tenting with a lake view.

Long-term monthly users take many of the better sites. Sites #23 and 25 are right by the steps to the beach.

The view from the lakeshore sites is dramatic. Be sure to bring a folding chair for everyone.

If you call to make a reservation, the helpful staff will get you into the best possible site.

OPERATED BY
City of Two Harbors

OPEN
Mid-May to late October.

SITES
102 RV sites with electricity and water, including 36 with sewer. 10 primitive tent sites.

GETTING A SITE
Register at office. Reservations accepted.

RESERVATIONS
Call (218) 834-2021. Leave a message during the off-season.

FACILITIES
Flush toilets, drinking water, showers, dump station.

FEES
$18 per tent, $24-$26 for RV. Extra charge for extra vehicles, tents. Credit cards accepted.

CONTACT
Burlington Bay Campground
City of Two Harbors
522 First Avenue
Two Harbors, MN 55616
www.ci.two-harbors.mn.us/
and visit "City Departments"

Site #48 at Burlington Bay is a typical shoreline site, with great views but little privacy.

Burlington Bay Campground

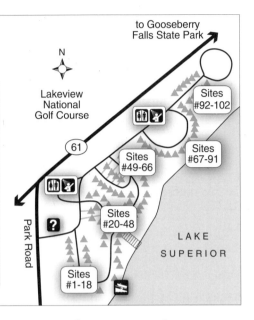

to Gooseberry
Falls State Park

N

Lakeview
National
Golf Course

61

Park Road

Sites
#92-102

Sites
#67-91

Sites
#49-66

Sites
#20-48

Sites
#1-18

LAKE

SUPERIOR

GETTING THERE

The campground is on the east side of Two Harbors. From the west (Duluth), travel through town on Seventh Avenue. Just past the R.J. Houle information center, turn right on Park Road then enter campground on the left.

You'll enjoy these activities & features

★ Hiking: Sonju Trail

★ Walk to town

★ Lakeshore sites
   (on Lake Superior)

★ Lake Superior access

★ Golf at Superior National across the highway, a campers' store, etc.

From the campground you can walk the Sonju Trail, which circles Lighthouse Point and brings you to the Agate Bay harbor area. There you can watch ships being loaded with taconite, tour the Two Harbors Lighthouse, or go onboard the historic *Edna G.* tugboat.

Some trivia for the campfire: Burlington Bay was the site of the original Township of Burlington, which incorporated in 1857. It was a separate town until 1894 when it merged with the Township of Agate Bay to form the town of Two Harbors.

Burlington Bay

Explore Lighthouse Point

By foot or by bike, Lighthouse Point is a great destination for the explorers in your group. From the campground, cross the beach area on Park Road and then connect with the Sonju Trail. This wide trail runs just over a half mile through beautiful Lakeview Park all the way to Lighthouse Point. There you'll find a wide rock beach for wave watching or puddle dipping and of course the lighthouse itself. The **Two Harbors Lighthouse** is open for visits seven days a week in the summer. Feeling brave? Walk out on the break wall with its skimpy fence and take in all of Agate Bay, with its massive ore docks. If you're lucky, a 1000-ft. ship might be in port loading taconite. As one billboard promoting the town used to say, "Watch great ladies get loaded in Two Harbors." Visit www.twoharborschamber.com for more information.

Spend a day in Two Harbors

The "two harbors" in Two Harbors are 1) Burlington Bay, where the campground is, and 2) Agate Bay, where downtown and the ore docks are. Lighthouse Point separates the two bays. Two Harbors could also be called "Two Main Streets," because over the decades the original main street has been nearly replaced by a new one.

The original main drag is First Avenue. When cars replaced the railroads for travelers, the main route through town moved up to Seventh Avenue. Now, the First Avenue downtown area has the cultural attractions, and Seventh Avenue is home to the tourist businesses.

Civic boosters have tried for years to get more people downtown. Do the boosters a favor: go experience the downtown waterfront. Tour the historic tugboat *Edna G.*, visit the **3M/Dwan Museum**, with its history of the North Shore origins of Minnesota Mining, and check out the **Lake County Historical Depot Museum,** with an interactive map of Lake County. There's even a retail shop or two to visit.

Walk down Highway 61 into town and hit the Seventh Avenue main drag. **The Vanilla Bean** is a great restaurant and bakery. **Dairy Queen** is an obvious choice for a sweet treat, but how about pie at **Judy's Café** or something off the dessert menu at **Black Woods?** Hikers should be sure to drop in at the Superior Hiking Trail Association office for the latest on this favorite hiking destination. There's a whole line-up of gift shops along Seventh Avenue, including an agate shop for a unique North Shore souvenir.

Indian Lake Brimson, Minnesota

This campground takes full advantage of Indian Lake, with quiet waterfront sites and a boat launch. From the dock, look back at the swimming beach and lakeshore sites. Escape from Duluth for a quick overnight or stay here for a week—you'll find this campground suited to both kinds of getaways.

A SHORT DRIVE FROM THE BUSY NORTH SHORE, Indian Lake campground is a nice overnight getaway on a quiet scenic lake, ringed by red and jack pines. The campground site used to be an Ojibwe settlement and a former Brimson community club.

Sites #21-25 on Loop A are beautiful carry-in lakeshore sites with a bit of gravel beach at mid-summer. They even have their own hand pump for water. If you have a large rig, you'll find space in Loop B. Sites #9, 11, 12 and 13 on Loop B overlook the lake and have easy access to the boat ramp and scenic dock below. The swimming beach is sandy and shallow; bring your own horseshoes for the pits found there.

Sites are limited to eight people with two vehicles and two shelters. Maximum stay is 14 days.

Indian Lake is actually a wide spot in the Cloquet River, and you could paddle a canoe all the way downriver to the town of Cloquet from here.

In late July, you might get lucky and find this campground surrounded by ripe blueberry bushes. You won't be the first to pick the summer crop here; Ojibwe Indians did the same thing in centuries past.

OPERATED BY
Cloquet Valley State Forest

OPEN
May to October

SITES
25, plus group site.

GETTING A SITE
First-come, first-served. Choose a site, then register and pay at the registration station.

RESERVATIONS
None

FACILITIES
Vault toilet, hand water pumps.

FEES
$12

CONTACT
Managed by Split Rock Lighthouse State Park
(218) 226-6377

You'll enjoy these activities & features

★ Canoeing
★ Fishing: panfish, northern pike
★ Swimming: at beach
★ Boat ramp
★ Lakeshore sites (on Indian Lake)
★ Handicapped accessible sites

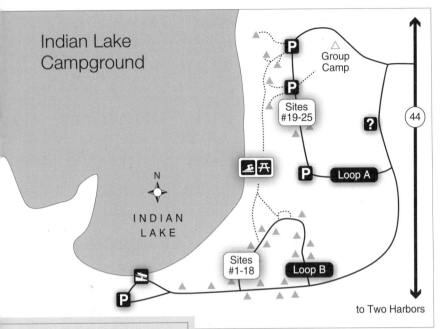

Indian Lake Campground

Group Camp

Sites #19-25

44

Loop A

N

INDIAN LAKE

Sites #1-18

Loop B

to Two Harbors

GETTING THERE

From Two Harbors, take County Road 2 north for 13 miles to County Road 14. Turn left on 14. This road turns into St. Louis County Road 55. Drive 10.2 miles total to County Road 44 and turn right, by Hugo's Bar. Take County Road 44 1.2 miles north to campground entrance on left.

Site #21 is one of five walk-in sites right on the water's edge.

Pick blueberries

Berry season is hard to predict precisely on the calendar, so don't schedule your entire northern Minnesota camping trip around berry picking. But if you're on the North Shore between mid-July and mid-August, there will be berries somewhere. If the bears don't get them first, why not pick a quart or two for yourself? The North Shore is renowned for its delicious and usually abundant wild blueberries.

Indian Lake is named for the native people who used to visit this area every year to pick berries. The Ojibwe Indians were seasonal migrants, so families made camps around the region at different times of the year and for different types of food gathering. Spring food gathering was at a maple syrup sugar bush, late summer was for wild rice, and fall was the time for a hunting camp. Mid-summer food gathering focused on picking berries. Blueberries could be picked by the bushel and then dried for the winter.

The Indian Lake campground has perfect conditions for blueberries—the soil is sandy, well-drained, and slightly acidic due to the conifer trees. There are blueberry plants scattered around the campground. If you're here in late July or early August, look around. You might just find a special sweet treat for your camp stove pancakes, or enough to take home for ice cream.

Another favorite place to pick blueberries on the North Shore is at **Palisade Head**, in Tettegouche State Park. Or stop in at a Superior National Forest ranger station in Tofte or Grand Marais and ask for advice. Many places along the Superior Hiking Trail have awesome berries; ask at the SHTA office in Two Harbors.

If the blueberries aren't ripe, look for raspberries, wild strawberries, or the elusive thimbleberry.

Gooseberry Falls
State Park Two Harbors, Minnesota

Gooseberry Falls is the most popular state park on the North Shore—camp here for a couple of days and learn why. The fabulous waterfalls just off the paved trail at the Visitors Center are only the beginning. Take a different hike every day, ride your bike to Split Rock, or just hang out on the Lake Superior shore.

GORP.COM RATES GOOSEBERRY FALLS STATE PARK as one of the top ten camping sites in the country. Direct access to the park's wide network of trails and beautiful lakeshore will keep you busy for days. This campground has the most beautiful picnic area and the most beautiful bathroom/shower building on the North Shore.

There are four loops, each with their own character. The upper loops (sites #1-44) are in more open woods and get some highway noise. The lower two loops (sites #45-70) are more wooded. Lakeshore sites #58 and 59, which can be reserved, are popular, and they provide access to a rocky but private shoreline. Site #61, which is available only a first-come, first-served basis, is the only site with direct access to the lakeshore. None of the sites have a view of the lake, at least during summer when the trees are in leaf.

If you really want to camp right on the lakeshore, arrive by bike or by foot and register for one of the three bike/hike sites in the "Davis Area," a 150 yard walk in from the beautiful bathhouse.

No visit to this campground would be complete without having one of your meals out on Picnic Flow, a wide expanse of bare bedrock sloping down into the lake. It's only labeled on the maps and signs as "Picnic Area," but it's gorgeous. You can reach the picnic area from trails that lead from any of the loops.

OPERATED BY
Minnesota State Parks

OPEN
Year-round. Limited facilities November to April.

SITES
70, plus two group sites. Vehicle length limit 40 ft.

GETTING A SITE
47 sites are reservable, 23 sites are first-come, first-served. Check in at the registration station along the entrance road.

RESERVATIONS
Visit www.stayatmnparks.com or call (866) 85PARKS.

FACILITIES
Vault and flush toilets, drinking water, showers, dump station.

FEES
$18, plus state park permit.

CONTACT
Gooseberry Falls State Park
3206 Highway 61 East
Two Harbors, MN 55616
(218) 834-3855
www.dnr.state.mn.us/state_parks/gooseberry_falls

You'll enjoy these activities & features

★ Hiking
★ Fishing: brook trout, spring steelhead, fall salmon
★ Swimming: at river mouth
★ Sea kayaking
★ Lake Superior access
★ State park naturalist programs and store
★ Handicapped accessible sites (#43, 44)

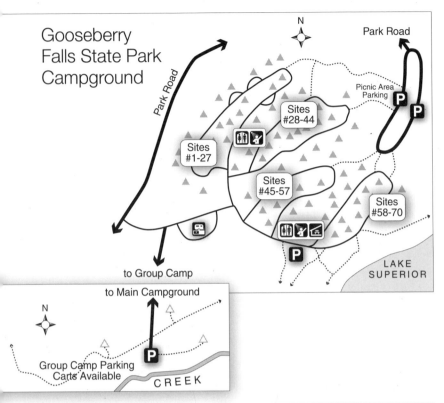

Gooseberry Falls State Park Campground

Park Road

N

Park Road

Picnic Area Parking

Sites #28-44

Sites #1-27

Sites #45-57

Sites #58-70

LAKE SUPERIOR

to Group Camp

to Main Campground

N

to Main Campground

Group Camp Parking
Carts Available

CREEK

GETTING THERE

The entrance to Gooseberry Falls State Park is on the Lake Superior side at Milepost 39.5, 13 miles northeast of Two Harbors. Turn to the right off the main entrance road 0.2 miles from Highway 61. The registration station is a small building along the road to the lakeshore. A state park permit is required on this road, which means that you will leave behind the crowds at the waterfalls as soon as you turn off the main entrance road.

A meal at Picnic Flow is a must-do for Gooseberry campers.

Ride the Gitchi-Gami State Trail

What a great idea! Build a paved trail next to Highway 61 from Two Harbors to Grand Marais, connecting five great state parks and eight or ten towns along the way.

The snowmobilers have their trail deep in the woods, and hikers have the Superior Hiking Trail along the North Shore's famous ridgeline. Like both of these trails, the Gitchi-Gami Trail is something special. Most state bike trails were built on old railroad beds, which makes for flat, straight trails. Not this one. It's curvy and hilly and a lot of fun.

The trail was originally planned to be built into the old curves of Highway 61 as the highway was rebuilt and straightened out. For example, the old Highway 61 road around Silver Creek Cliff was abandoned when the Silver Creek tunnel was built through the rock. Now you can bike (or walk) on the Gitchi-Gami trail up to the incredible viewpoint left when the highway was rerouted.

From Gooseberry Falls State Park, you can now ride your bike all the way past **Split Rock Lighthouse** to downtown Beaver Bay. Currently, this 13-mile section is the longest stretch of completed bike trail. And it's gorgeous country. The trail follows the highway but also heads off into wild country never before accessible to the public. Be sure to stop at **Twin Points Public Water Access** and hike out to **Iona's Beach Scientific and Natural Area**, a unique red rhyolite shingle beach. In Split Rock Lighthouse State Park, the trail winds and rolls like no other paved trail in the state. Take another break at the Split Rock's trail center and the great beach there. In Beaver Bay, stop for ice cream at the **Big Dipper** before starting the long trip back.

Other sections of the trail completed include a nice stretch through Schroeder and Tofte, a short bit of trail near Grand Marais, and the very scenic half mile around Silver Creek Cliff. Plans call for new trail in the Silver Bay to Beaver Bay and Lutsen areas.

For current trail conditions, contact the Gitchi-Gami Trail Association at www.ggta.org or the Minnesota DNR at www.dnr.state.mn.us/state_trails

Split Rock Lighthouse State Park Beaver Bay, Minnesota

How's this for a campsite view? Cart-in camping at Split Rock provides peace and quiet with incredible views and all the comforts of hot showers and nice hiking trail systems.

WOW. TALK ABOUT NORTH SHORE CAMPING. If you can manage camping a short walk away from your car, you'll find some of the area's best camping experiences here. In fact, the DNR's *Minnesota Conservation Volunteer* magazine named this one of the top four state park campgrounds in the state.

The campground is full almost every night from mid-May to October, so you have to plan ahead, especially if you have a favorite site.

Three or four of the sites are within an easy stroll from the parking area, but for the rest you'll want to use the carts that are provided to haul your gear to your site. The walking distance in to the sites ranges from 350 ft. to 1,950 ft. Each site has its own cart with the site number on it, and you pick up the key to unlock the cart when you register. Although the lakeshore sites may be desirable for their views, the inland sites are just as nice and provide protection from cold lake breezes, steep cliffs and shoreline flies.

If you don't have a reservation, show up at the campground office early in the morning (preferably when it opens at 8:30 a.m.), to get on a waiting list for that day's openings. In the off-season (late October to April) all sites are available on a first-come, first-served basis.

If you want a lakeshore site, a reservation is a must. The six non-reservable sites (sites #5-10) are all away from the lake, in a tidy little valley. Lakeshore sites often have a sitting bench near the lake to enjoy the views.

Site #4 is just 400 feet from the parking lot and very convenient to the restrooms. Long-time North Shore state park manager Paul Sundberg has

OPERATED BY
Minnesota State Parks

OPEN
Year-round, but limited restroom facilities Oct. to May.

SITES
20, all cart-in

GETTING A SITE
14 sites are reservable, 6 are first-come, first-served. Reservations strongly recommended. Check in at the park office.

RESERVATIONS
Visit www.stayatmnparks.com or call (866) 85PARKS.

FACILITIES
Vault toilets near campsites, showers, drinking water and flush toilets at parking area

FEES
$18, plus state park permit.

CONTACT
Split Rock Lighthouse State Park
3755 Split Rock Lighthouse Rd.
Two Harbors, MN 55616
(218) 226-6377
www.dnr.state.mn.us/state_parks/split_rock_lighthouse

You'll enjoy these activities & features

★ Hiking
★ Lakeshore sites (on Lake Superior)
★ Lake Superior access
★ Interpretive and historical programs at Lighthouse
★ Handicapped accessible sites (#2, 3)

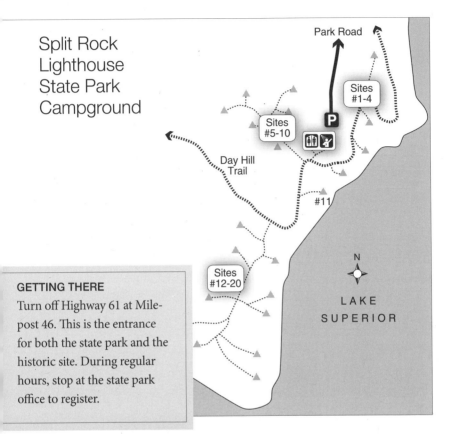

Split Rock Lighthouse State Park Campground

Park Road

Sites #1-4

P

Sites #5-10

Day Hill Trail

#11

Sites #12-20

N

LAKE SUPERIOR

GETTING THERE
Turn off Highway 61 at Milepost 46. This is the entrance for both the state park and the historic site. During regular hours, stop at the state park office to register.

Unlock your own cart at the parking lot and head out to your campsite.

said it's his favorite site at his favorite campground, with a terrific view of the lighthouse.

Site #11 is tucked into a rocky hillside and is next to a unique beach of large cobblestones. It's the most visible of the sites from the cart trail.

Site #13 has access to the same cobblestone beach.

Site #15, away from the lakeshore, has its own private giant boulder, good for climbing.

Sites #16-19 are situated above a high cliff and don't provide direct lake access, just great views. Site #18 has a particularly dramatic view of Split Rock Lighthouse.

Site #20 is the longest haul, but rewards you with privacy and a nice view to the southwest down the shore. Follow the Day Hill Trail from here down 130 foot steps to a dramatic private beach.

While camping here, you have all of Split Rock Lighthouse State Park to explore. The park has miles of hiking trails, including dramatic sections of the Superior Hiking Trail. Bring your bikes and ride the rolling, hilly Gitchi-Gami bike trail east to Beaver Bay or west to Gooseberry Falls State Park. And of course, you can enjoy at least a half-day at the lighthouse itself, with guided tours, the museum with a movie, and just taking in the view.

This beautiful cobblestone beach is right next to site #11.

Visit the lighthouse

Over 120,000 people visit Split Rock Lighthouse every year. The lighthouse is an icon for Minnesota and the North Shore—it was even considered for use on the Minnesota state quarter.

It adds a special twist to a lighthouse tour to know that, like the keepers, you live here. Maybe your campsite has a view of the lighthouse; look back from the lighthouse fence and see your site up on top of that cliff. Those tourists will be back in the motel tonight watching "Sponge Bob" reruns while you're making hot cocoa with the lighthouse as your backdrop.

The lighthouse is part of a 25-acre historic site managed by the Minnesota Historical Society. It's open every day from 10–6. Admission to the site is $8 for adults, with discounts for children, seniors and college students. You'll find a very nice exhibit about lighthouses, North Shore history, and more. The short film is emotionally powerful. Guides in period costume take you around the site. Be sure to climb the stairs to the top of the lighthouse. Hang out on the top as long as possible. After all, you live here now.

Hike the Superior Hiking Trail

One of the most popular sections of the Superior Hiking Trail is nearby. The loop around the Split Rock River is a five-mile trail that takes you through a nice variety of terrain. You can drive to the trailhead, or hike 1.5 miles from the campground.

If you want to get away from the crowds and have more of a challenge, take the 11-mile hike to Beaver Bay. This is a great section of the SHT, with tough hills, terrific views and nice forests. From the campground, use a park map to follow the park's hiking/ski trails past Day Hill and across Highway 61 to cut up to the SHT proper. If you plan correctly and make advance reservations, the Superior Shuttle can bring you right back to the campground.

For information on the Superior Hiking Trail and the Superior Shuttle, see next page.

THE SUPERIOR HIKING TRAIL

Are you a hiker who likes to camp? A camper who likes to hike? The Superior Hiking Trail (SHT) is a world-class hiking trail that features the best of the North Shore's dramatic terrain and wild landscapes.

The SHT connects most of the North Shore state parks along its 250-mile route between Duluth and the Canadian border. It leads right to eight of the campgrounds in this book, and seven more campgrounds are within a few miles of a SHT trailhead.

The SHT is a foot-traffic-only trail that winds along the ridgeline that parallels Lake Superior. Trailheads are located at major road intersections, in the state parks, and at spur trails that connect to lakeshore towns and resorts. The trail is well-marked and well-maintained. It's been named one of the top 10 long-distance trails in the country; a trail that "leaves the others in the dust."

Campgrounds with direct access to SHT:

- Jay Cooke State Park
- Gooseberry Falls State Park
- Split Rock Lighthouse State Park
- Tettegouche State Park
- Lamb's Resort
- Temperance River State Park
- Cascade River State Park
- Judge C.R. Magney State Park

Three campgrounds are perfect for hiking the SHT. The cart-in campground at **Split Rock Lighthouse State Park** is tucked in a network of trails connected to great stretches of the SHT. The Split Rock River loop is one of the most popular parts of the trail, and the trail to Beaver Bay is remote and dramatic. The drive-in campground at **Tettegouche State Park** puts you right next to two of the most dramatic parts of the trail, west to Bean and Bear Lakes and east through the Wolf Ridge area. **Cascade River State Park** is truly a hiker's park—hike the Cascade River loop or summit Lookout Mountain.

Be sure to check the schedule for the **Superior Shuttle.** This is a private business that transports hikers from one trailhead to another between Two Harbors and Grand Marais, allowing hikers to hike back to their car (or campground). With prior reservations, the shuttle may be able to pick you up right in your campground and drive you to a trailhead. From that starting spot, you simply hike back to your campsite.

If you're planning to hike the SHT, check in at the Superior Hiking Trail Association office in Two Harbors. They can provide current trail conditions, supply you with maps, and even sell you a useful logo T-shirt or water bottle—and all SHT store purchases support this great trail.

FOR MORE INFORMATION www.shta.org | www.superiorhikingshuttle.com

Eighteen Lake Isabella, Minnesota

Remote and quiet Eighteen Lake will capture your heart. Carry your canoe down these wooden steps and have the small lake to yourself. Camp under the towering pines, draw water from the lake...it's all free for you to enjoy.

THIS IS RUSTIC AND QUIET CAMPING in a shady forest of white and red pine. Each pull-through site has a picnic bench, fire grate, and at least one tent pad. The three sites aren't numbered, and it's first-come, first-served.

Eighteen Lake is a quiet, piney lake, with a maximum depth of 12 feet. Bring your own drinking water and pack out your own garbage for this near-wilderness experience. Crafty campers will bring a bucket and use the lake water for clean-up.

A 2.7 mile hiking trail circles Eighteen Lake, with four overlooks. The first overlook going south is just 0.2 miles from the campground, so it would be an easy and rewarding trek even for small children.

In numerous visits to this campground, it has been quiet and pristine. Unlike some national forest rustic campgrounds, Eighteen Lake seems to attract more hikers and scenery-seekers than anglers and the campsites smell like pine trees, not fish.

If you do come to fish, walk or drive back across Forest Road 369 and follow the rough road and trail to Redskin (or Indian) Lake, a designated trout lake. Bring a good map: Spear Lake, Weapon Lake and Trappers Lake are also nearby and have brook trout.

Eighteen Lake is the closest campground to BWCA entry points around Isabella Lake, including the Pow-Wow Hiking Trail, so you might stay here a night before the big trip.

OPERATED BY
Superior National Forest

OPEN
May to October

SITES
3

GETTING A SITE
First-come, first-served

RESERVATIONS
None

FACILITIES
Vault toilet (no water).

FEES
Free

CONTACT
Tofte Ranger District
PO Box 2159, Tofte MN 55615
(218) 663-8060
www.fs.fed.us/r9/superior
E-mail: tofte@fs.fed.us

You'll enjoy these activities & features
★ Canoeing
★ Fishing: walleye, perch
★ Hiking

Eighteen Lake Campground

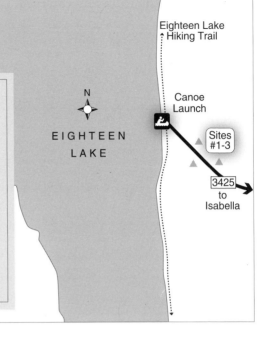

GETTING THERE

From Finland, take Highway 1 a winding 16 miles to Isabella. Turn right (east) on Forest Road 172 (Wanless Road). After 0.8 miles, turn left (north) on Forest Road 369 (Sawbill Landing Road). After 1.6 miles, turn left on Forest Road 3425 at sign for Eighteen Lake Recreation Site. Campground and lake are 0.6 miles in.

NATIONAL FOREST "RUSTIC CAMPGROUND" CAMPING

- Pack it in, pack it out. These campgrounds have no garbage service, so bring a bag for garbage and another for recyclables.

- Most have no water pump. You can filter the lake water for drinking and collect it for washing dishes back at camp. Or bring water in jugs.

- Something may be fishy—these campgrounds are popular with anglers. Unfortunately, anglers are sometimes careless enough to leave fish guts around the campsite and in the fire pits, and the whole area can smell.

- These campsites have a picnic table, a fire pit, and room for a tent. Pop-up trailers generally work well, but there often isn't room for an RV.

- Don't count on toilet paper in the vault toilets. The Forest Service can't always keep up with the maintenance. Bring your own.

Hike the "Lake District"

England's Lake District is a beautiful and popular destination for hikers because of its mountains and lakes. Did you know we have our own "Lake District" right here on the North Shore? You'll find hiking trails around scenic lakes and over mountain-like terrain—a lot closer to home.

Forest Road (FR) 172 connects three lake trails. You could hike around a different lake each day, or do all three trails for a total of about nine miles of hiking. Call or visit the Tofte Ranger Station before setting out, to make sure all the trails are passable. This is remote country and these trails won't be the first ones cleared after a storm.

The Eighteen Lake campground is the trailhead for the **Eighteen Lake Trail**, a 2.7 mile trail. This trail is known for its varied habitat. Watch for moose as you wind through cedar groves and tall pine.

The **Divide Lake Trail** also starts from a campground, the small Divide Lake campground. From Eighteen Lake, return on FR 369 to FR 172, turn east (left) for 4.2 miles to the campground on the right. The trail leads 2.1 miles around Divide Lake.

Continue another seven miles along FR 172 to the Hogback Lake Recreation Area. There's another nice campground here, a "rustic" campground like Eighteen Lake with three sites. The **Hogback Lake Trail** is actually a small trail system that circles Scarp Lake and visits two other little lakes. The loop around Scarp makes a 3.2 mile hike up and down bedrock ridges called "hogbacks." If this is your last hike of the day, start with a picnic lunch in the scenic picnic area nestled under the white pines.

FOR MORE INFORMATION, check out "50 Circuit Hikes" by Howard Fenton, which describes all these hikes in detail.

Eckbeck Little Marais, Minnesota

Illgen Falls on the Baptism River is about a mile from the Eckbeck campground. It's the same Baptism River that flows past the campground, but here it's a scenic wonder.

THE BAPTISM RIVER is a classic North Shore stream, and you can enjoy it fully at this campground.

Only sites #18 and 19 are right on the river. Sites #11, 13, 15 and 16 are the nicest; they are on the outer edge of the campground, near the river and more private than the others. The rest of the sites are fairly exposed, with little visual privacy between sites.

But all the sites have easy access to the large riverside picnic area. Take your breakfast or dinner down to the picnic area and enjoy the gurgling river.

The campground water supply is a bit unusual. It's an artesian spring, which just runs and runs.

Sites are limited to eight people with two vehicles and two shelters. Maximum stay is 14 days.

Take a pleasant walk or short drive of 1.2 miles down the highway to Illgen Falls, a high waterfall on the Baptism River. The Superior Hiking Trail has a trailhead about 2 miles away, for the "Highway 1 to Lake County Road 6" section. This is a dramatic and challenging 6.8 mile hike. If your group includes a non-hiker, then you're set for a shuttle to the other end of the trail on County Road 6. For an easier hike that doesn't need a shuttle, climb up the first mile to the "Fantasia" overlooks.

In spring, experienced whitewater paddlers take canoes and kayaks from the Finland campground to this one, 5.2 miles on the Baptism River with Class I to Class III rapids.

Here's some typo trivia for the campfire: Illgen Falls is named after the Rudolph Ilgen family that settled here in 1924. And the Baptism River was originally called the Baptist river.

OPERATED BY
Finland State Forest

OPEN
May to October

SITES
30. Vehicle length limit 45 ft.

GETTING A SITE
First-come, first-served. Choose an open site, then register and pay at the station near entrance.

RESERVATIONS
None

FACILITIES
Vault toilets, artesian spring water.

FEES
$12

CONTACT
Managed by
Tettegouche State Park
5702 Highway 61
Silver Bay, Minnesota 55614
(218) 226-6365

You'll enjoy these activities & features

★ Canoeing
★ Fishing: brook trout
★ Hiking
★ Riverside sites (on Baptism River)
★ Handicapped accessible sites

Eckbeck Campground

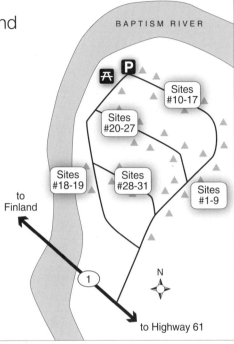

BAPTISM RIVER

Sites #10-17

Sites #20-27

Sites #18-19

Sites #28-31

Sites #1-9

to Finland

1

N

to Highway 61

GETTING THERE

From Highway 61 Milepost 60.2, take Highway 1 for 2.7 miles to campground entrance on right. Or follow Highway 1 for 3.0 miles south from downtown Finland.

WHAT TO DO ON RAINY DAYS

- **Go for a drive.** Visit a new lake down a new road and explore the great North Shore.

- **Visit a museum:** Try Split Rock Lighthouse, Great Lakes Aquarium in Duluth, the North Shore Commercial Fishing Museum in Tofte, or Grand Portage National Monument.

- **Keep the campfire burning.** It's easier to keep a fire alive than start it from wet coals.

- **Go shopping.** You could spend hours in the Silver Bay shopping center, Grand Marais' downtown, Duluth's Canal Park area, or the Beaver Bay Minimall.

- **Go swimming...indoors.** Find your nearest resort or hotel with a pool; often they'll let you use the pool, whirlpool, and sauna for a minimal per person charge.

Fish the Baptism River

 The rugged landscape of the North Shore means there's a huge diversity of landscapes and habitats. That's true for hikers, campers…and fish.

Most of the campgrounds in this book have some sort of fishing right at the campground. Eckbeck and Finland are two of the few campgrounds situated on a river, not on a lake. And river fishing is completely different from lake fishing.

North Shore rivers can each be divided into two sections: above the "barrier" and below the "barrier." The barrier is generally one of those dramatic waterfalls we all love, like Gooseberry Falls on the Gooseberry River or the High Falls of the Baptism River. These falls stop all upstream fish traffic, so the fish found in the river above the "barrier" live there year-round. Below the barrier, at the mouths of the rivers, all kinds of interesting things happen fish-wise, as fish that spend most of their lives in the open waters of Lake Superior take turns coming up the river to spawn.

At Eckbeck and Finland campgrounds, the Baptism River is above a lot of barriers, including nearby scenic Illgen Falls. So the only fish here are the resident stream trout, the brook trout and brown trout.

According to the Department of Natural Resources (DNR), the resident "brookies" are small, just 6-15 inches. You can fish for these using a very simple spinning rod. For lures, the DNR recommends either tiny spinners or angleworms.

Fly fishers also frequent North Shore rivers, including the Baptism, whose wide, open bed is good for the long casts of fly fishing.

Anglers age 16 and over need a state license to fish, plus a "trout stamp" to fish in the Baptism River or other designated trout streams. You can buy the license and a virtual stamp at any Electronic Licensing Systems outlet (including the bait shops in Finland and most gas stations along Highway 61), online, or by calling the DNR at (888) 665-4236.

FOR MORE INFORMATION on North Shore fishing, check out books from resident Shawn Perich: "Fly-Fishing the North Country" and "Fishing Lake Superior."

Finland Finland, Minnesota

The Baptism River cuts right across the Finland campground.
This footbridge connects the campground with a picnic area and the
restaurants and stores of downtown Finland.

WITH PRIVATE SITES and a lot of nearby activities, this is a perfect
location for extended stays, with bustling Finland a short walk away
and a scenic eight mile drive down to Tettegouche or Little Marais
on Lake Superior.

The campground is popular with family groups in tents and the
occasional tent trailer or small RV. Sites #5, 7, and 8 back up to the
Baptism River. Sites #13 and 14 have a great rock wall for kids to climb.

Sites #25-29 are separate from the rest of the campground, down a short road that leads to the footbridge. Sites #27 and 28 are right on the river's edge. They are in an open field and are best used by groups or families. In fact these sites can be reserved ahead of time by groups by contacting Tettegouche State Park.

Cross the Baptism River on a nice footbridge and explore the picnic area, where the west and east branches of the Baptism come together. Then continue into Finland for dinner or for shopping at the all-purpose Finland Co-op.

Sites are limited to eight people with two vehicles and two shelters. Maximum stay is 14 days.

The Finland campground is only a few miles away from Eckbeck campground, and it's on the same river. Which campground is best for you? This campground offers much more privacy. It's an easy walk to fun areas like the picnic area between two branches of the Baptism and to shopping. Eckbeck has better river access and is a few miles closer to hiking trails and the dramatic shoreline of Tettegouche.

OPERATED BY
Finland State Forest

OPEN
May to October

SITES
39, including one group site. Vehicle length limit 50 ft.

GETTING A SITE
First-come, first-served. Choose an open site, then register and pay at station near entrance.

RESERVATIONS
None, except group site.

FACILITIES
Vault toilet, hand water pump.

FEES
$12

CONTACT
Tettegouche State Park
5702 Highway 61
Silver Bay, Minnesota 55614
(218) 226-6365

You'll enjoy these activities & features

★ Fishing: brook trout
★ Walking to town
★ Riverside sites (Baptism River)
★ Handicapped accessible sites (#9 and 12)

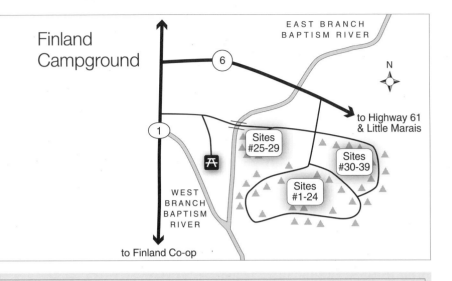

Finland
Campground

EAST BRANCH
BAPTISM RIVER

6

N

to Highway 61
& Little Marais

1

Sites
#25-29

Sites
#30-39

Sites
#1-24

WEST
BRANCH
BAPTISM
RIVER

to Finland Co-op

GETTING THERE

From Highway 61 at Milepost 65, take County Road 6 (Little Marais Road) 7.9 miles to campground entrance on left. Or, from Finland, take County Road 6 0.2 miles to campground entrance.

Site #2 is a typical Finland campsite—nice for tenting, private, and with room to explore.

Explore Crosby-Manitou State Park

Quick, count all the North Shore state parks! From Jay Cooke to Grand Portage, there are nine parks, but many people forget about one of them: George H. Crosby-Manitou State Park. From the Finland campground, you're at a great starting point for exploring this wilderness giant. Pack a lunch and head up the Cramer Road for a day of adventure.

Crosby-Manitou State Park straddles the deep gorge of the Manitou River. It's not as well known as other parks because there's no access off of Highway 61. But if you like to hike and explore wild areas, this is for you. To reach the park, drive County Road 7 seven miles out of Finland, a lovely drive up the east fork of the Baptism River. The park entrance is on the right. This gets you to the trailhead.

Four trails leave from the trailhead area, and you can find three or four excellent loop hikes from here. Be sure to find your way down to the **Manitou River**. Manitou is the Ojibwe word for "spirit," and this river is full of spirit. And brook trout.

There is camping in the state park, but it's all backpacking sites. There are several sites on **Benson Lake** that are only a few hundred yards from the parking lot, but even these are rough and rustic. The park is managed by Tettegouche State Park, so if you're headed this way, check in there for a trail map and any updates.

Explore Finland

Finland, Minnesota, population around 600, is not incorporated as a town, but is the buzzing urban center of Silver Creek Township. There's a wide cast of characters in the environs, ranging from funky environmental educators from **Wolf Ridge Environmental Learning Center** to the descendents of Finnish pioneers. The **Finland Co-op** is the economic center of town, but the three bars keep busy, too. You probably won't be camping here on the day before Saint Patrick's Day, but that's the busiest day of the year as Finns and friends from across the region come to celebrate St. Urho's Day.

From the Finland campground, it's an easy walk across the Baptism River bridge, past the picnic area and into town. You can make a phone call, stock up at the Co-op, or engage a local in a political conversation; you never know what you'll hear!

Ninemile Lake Finland, Minnesota

Pretty Ninemile Lake can be the ace up your sleeve. Despite attractive campsites and ample activities nearby, the campground almost always has an open site.

WHEN IT'S CROWDED ON THE North Shore itself, take a scenic half-hour drive to Ninemile Lake and you'll probably find a site at this spacious campground. Of the 26 sites, eleven are on the shore of the attractive lake. Waterfront sites are #16-26, and you should grab one of these if you can. Although you can't see much of the lake from these sites, each one has its own bit of waterfront down a short path, with its own wooden steps.

Throughout the campground, all the sites are private and spacious. A foot trail through cedar and pine along the lake connects the shoreline sites with the boat landing, where there is a sturdy dock.

You could swim here, but it's a bit weedy in mid-summer.

Ninemile Lake is experiencing a lot of development pressure, with a newly rebuilt "Village at Nine Mile" bringing new cabins and a new restaurant. But the campground is well situated for privacy and scenic views.

A half-mile hiking trail starts across the county road from the campground and leads to a nice overview of the area.

A few miles drive up County Road 7 takes you to more lakes for fishing or paddling, and to the Trestle Inn at the Crooked Lake Resort, a full-service restaurant in the middle of the National Forest, perfect for lunch or dinner on a rainy day.

Some trivia for the campfire: according to local legend, Ninemile Lake got its name because it was a nine mile journey in from the Lake Superior shore along the historic Pork Bay Trail. This trail was used by fur traders and native Americans, connecting the big lake with the inland waterways.

OPERATED BY
Superior National Forest

OPEN
Full services mid-May to September 30.

SITES
26. Vehicle length limit 50 ft.

GETTING A SITE
First-come, first-served. Choose an open site, then register and pay at station near entrance.

RESERVATIONS
None

FACILITIES
Vault toilets, solar water pump.

FEES
$12

CONTACT
Tofte Ranger District
PO Box 2159, Tofte MN 55615
(218) 663-8060
www.fs.fed.us/r9/superior

You'll enjoy these activities & features

★ Canoeing
★ Hiking
★ Fishing: walleye, northern
★ Boat ramp
★ Lakeshore sites (on Ninemile Lake)
★ Canoe rental & firewood may be available
★ Handicapped accessible sites

Ninemile Lake Campground

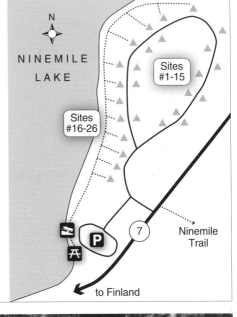

GETTING THERE

Reach the town of Finland from Highway 61 either on Highway 1 or Lake County Road 6. Follow Highway 1 north out of town, and on the edge of town turn right on Lake County Road 7. Follow Lake County Road 7 fifteen miles to campground on left. Campground is also accessible from Schroeder on Cook County Road 1 (Cramer Road), which turns into Lake County Road 8.

Sites #16-26 are arranged along Ninemile Lake and linked by a lakeshore trail.

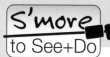

Hike the nearby trail

This is a national forest, and national forests are known as "Land of Many Uses." Once upon a time, eager recreation planners built a four-mile loop trail right here. But things change, and now there's just a half mile, dead-end trail. The remainder of the trail has seen active forestry operations.

The trail starts right across the road from the campground entrance. It climbs up to a maple forest ridgeline with a view into the Caribou River valley. Watch out for some confusing side trails.

Drive up the Cramer Road

Lake County Road 7 is also known as the "Cramer Road." It's named after the town of Cramer, named for J.N. Cramer, an early settler. You drove past Cramer on the way here, at the intersection of Lake County Road 7 and Lake County Road 8. There's not much left of this old railroad town, but once there were 8 to 10 homes here. Just to make things confusing, County Road 8 is also known as the Cramer Road, because it, too, led to the town of Cramer, from Schroeder. Of course, a road this straight through the wilderness wasn't built as a road, it was built as a logging railroad. And to top it off, Lake County Road 8 starts its life in Cook County, where it is known as Cook County Road 1.

But none of that matters now, because you're here. A drive further up County Road 7 can be a full day of adventure.

If you have a canoe or a fishing rod, you can pick from some mini-adventures. A few miles drive up County Road 7 takes you to more lakes for fishing or paddling. Sit by the shores of Echo Lake and fish for splake, carry your canoe a quarter mile into Goldeneye Lake for brook trout, or put in at Crooked Lake to paddle and portage the three-mile loop.

Keep going up County Road 7 for more adventures. A mile west on Forest Road 172 takes you to the **Hogback Lake Recreation Area**, where you can fish for trout from a pier or hike 3.2 miles around Scarp Lake. **Harriet Lake** is the location of a pioneer farm and still features open fields maintained for wildlife habitat. Stop in for some great birdwatching. Near the end of Cramer Road, turn left on Forest Road 354 and visit Kawishiwi Lake, right on the edge of the BWCA.

After these adventures, head to the **Trestle Inn** at the Crooked Lake Resort, a full-service restaurant in the middle of the National Forest, perfect for lunch or dinner on a rainy day.

Tettegouche
State Park <small>Silver Bay, Minnesota</small>

From the mouth of the Baptism River, check out the view of Shovel Point. The camping here is scenic and secluded, but the real attraction is the vast park itself, with ample hiking and adventure opportunities.

TETTEGOUCHE OFFERS TWO very different camping opportunities. The more traditional drive-in campground has the hot showers and convenience of most state parks, while the cart-in campground is nearly wilderness camping, with greater challenges and greater rewards.

The sites in the drive-in Baptism River Campground are private and shaded. You can't go wrong with any of them. There is no real view from any of them besides more woods. Sites #11, 13, 15, and

16 are just 200 feet from the Baptism River, but there is no easy access to the water. One writer referred to site #16 as "quaint." The most pleasant sites are the walk-in sites, where a 60-120 yard walk gets you privacy and a nice forest. If you like white pines, reserve walk-in site #7 or 25. A spur trail to the High Falls leads from site #19.

The cart-in Lake Superior Campground requires work. Park on the north side of the highway, load your cart, and haul your gear at least 500 yards to the sites. But the sites are excellent once you're there. Sites I, J and K have their own private beach. Site E is one of the closest and also sits right above the mouth of the Baptism River. Sites L, M and N are the farthest in but the least wild, located in an open field that was once the location of a tavern. There are outhouses at the cart-in area, but no drinking water. Drinking water and flush toilets are available at the park visitor center across the Baptism River bridge. For showers, drive up to the drive-in campground.

Tettegouche is popular among rock climbers. Shovel Point and Palisade Head challenge climbers with their 200-ft. cliffs.

OPERATED BY
Minnesota State Parks

OPEN
Year-round, but limited restroom facilities October–May.

SITES
28 sites at drive-in campground. Vehicle length limit 60 ft. 13 sites at cart-in campground. Two group sites.

GETTING A SITE
21 sites at drive-in campground are reservable; 7 are first-come, first-served. 10 sites at cart-in campground can be reserved; 3 are first-come, first-served. Reservations recommended. Check in at park office.

RESERVATIONS
Visit www.stayatmnparks.com or call (866) 85PARKS.

FACILITIES
Flush toilets, showers and drinking water at drive-in campground. Outhouses at cart-in campground. No water at cart-in or group campground.

FEES
$18 per night, plus state park permit.

CONTACT
Tettegouche State Park
5702 Highway 61
Silver Bay, Minnesota 55614
(218) 226-6365
www.dnr.state.mn.us/state_parks/Tettegouche

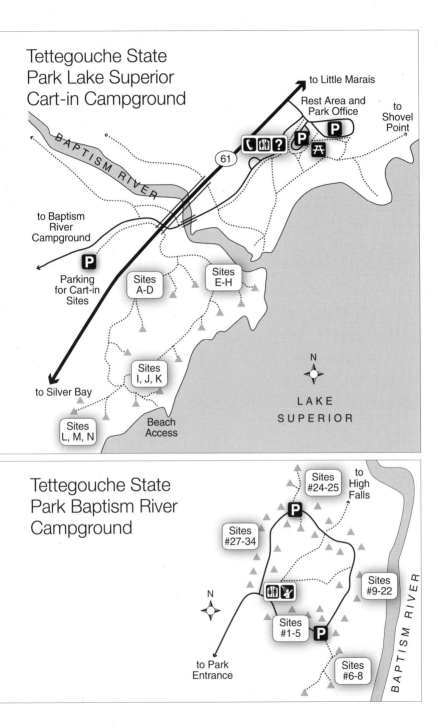

Tettegouche State
Park Lake Superior
Cart-in Campground

to Little Marais

Rest Area and
Park Office

to
Shovel
Point

61

to Baptism
River
Campground

Parking
for Cart-in
Sites

Sites
A-D

Sites
E-H

to Silver Bay

Sites
I, J, K

N

LAKE
SUPERIOR

Sites
L, M, N

Beach
Access

Tettegouche State
Park Baptism River
Campground

Sites
#24-25

to
High
Falls

Sites
#27-34

Sites
#9-22

N

Sites
#1-5

B A P T I S M   R I V E R

to Park
Entrance

Sites
#6-8

Cart-in site E sits right above the mouth of the Baptism River.

The scenic gorge of the Baptism River viewed from a park bridge.

You'll enjoy these activities & features

★ Hiking

★ Fishing: brook trout and salmon in Baptism River, trout in upper lakes

★ Swimming: at mouth of Baptism River

★ Lakeshore sites (Lake Superior sites in cart-in campground)

★ Lake Superior access

★ Handicapped accessible sites

GETTING THERE

The park is located at Highway 61 Milepost 58. Entrance to the park is 4.5 miles northeast of Silver Bay on Highway 61.

If you like to hike, Tettegouche State Park has it all. From rambles on wide, level trails to rugged long distance hikes, you'll find a trail to suit your hiking style. If you're camping here, you won't lack for adventures!

Take a short hike

Right out of the campground, by site #19, is a short trail to the **High Falls** of the Baptism River. This 60-foot drop is the highest waterfall within the borders of Minnesota (the High Falls of the Pigeon River in **Grand Portage State Park** are higher, but are shared with Ontario). The trail is less than one-half mile, and also leads to Two Step Falls. At the High Falls, the trail from the campground meets the Superior Hiking Trail. This trail crosses the river above the falls on a fancy suspension bridge. You can scamper down the other side of the river and see the falls from below.

From the park trailhead, which is just a short drive or walk from the campground at the end of the main park road, there are two short rambles up to overlooks. Follow the trail towards Nipisiquit Lake and turn off at the **Lake Superior Overlook** after about one mile.

Back at the lakeshore you'll find a classic but easy North Shore hike, out to **Shovel Point**. It's a bit rugged, but it offers an ever-changing view of dramatic Lake Superior cliffs with a fun overlook platform at the tip of rugged, rocky Shovel Point. If you're in the State Park Hiking Club, you'll find the secret password on this trail.

Take a long hike

Tettegouche State Park has a great trail network of its own, plus it's right in the heart of the most rugged country of the Superior Hiking Trail.

There's a challenging 6.8 mile loop trail around Mic Mac and Nipisiquit lakes and back on the Superior Hiking Trail that gets you to a wide variety of habitats and terrain. Highlights include **Tettegouche Camp**, where you can get out of the rain in the lodge building, and Conservancy Pines, a large stand of old-growth red pines down a short spur.

It's a rugged and dramatic seven mile hike one way to

Bean and Bear lakes west along the Superior Hiking Trail. You'll climb Mount Trudee and three or four other smaller summits along the way. Either return on this trail for a serious 15-mile day or arrange a shuttle (with the Superior Shuttle) to pick you up in Silver Bay.

FOR MORE INFORMATION on the Superior Hiking Trail, see page 33, visit www.shta.org or call (218) 834-2700. Contact the Superior Shuttle at (218) 834-5511.

(Below) Shovel Point can be seen through this arch at Tettegouche State Park.

Swim in the Baptism River

The mouth of the Baptism River is a favorite North Shore swimming hole. Warmer water from the river pools up before emptying into Lake Superior, so you get a nice cobblestone beach, beautiful lake views, and pleasant water temperature.

To reach the mouth of the river, drive or walk to the small parking lot between the park office and the old bridge. Head down the steps about 600 feet to the river mouth.

This is not an official swimming beach; there are no lifeguards. But folks have been swimming here forever.

Lamb's Resort Schroeder, Minnesota

Lamb's Resort has campsites right on the beautiful shoreline. Here you'll find some of the best lakeshore camping on the North Shore.

ENJOY THE LAST FAMILY-OWNED CAMPGROUND on the North Shore. While other campgrounds sell out and the land turns into condos, this one has been kept alive by the Lamb family through four generations, and you might see a young representative of generation five exploring the area.

Most of the sites have basic hook-ups available, and this campground is popular with RV campers. But there are some very nice tent sites that just happen to have utilities. Some of the best lakeshore locations on the North Shore are found at sites #1-8 and sites #50-59. Sites #50 and 51 back up to their own private cobblestone beach.

There really is something for the whole family here. There are video games, shopping, hiking, even hanging out at the pizza joint.

Even if you don't get a lakeshore site, it's still easy to get to the rocks and waves of Lake Superior.

Check out the sauna or scamper on the rocky but accessible shoreline. Too tired to cook? The Schroeder Baking Company will deliver a pizza to your campsite.

Lamb's Resort also has 14 cabins, so you can enjoy this unique site without camping gear.

OPERATED BY
Lamb's Resort

OPEN
May to October

SITES
74, all with water and electric hook-ups.

GETTING A SITE
Reservations recommended, but there is almost always a tent site available. Check in at the resort office just off of Highway 61.

RESERVATIONS
(218) 663-7292

FACILITIES
Flush and vault toilets, drinking water, showers, dump station.

FEES
$22-$33

CONTACT
Lamb's Resort, PO Box 415 Schroeder, MN 55613

You'll enjoy these activities & features

★ Hiking
★ Canoeing/sea kayaking
★ Fishing: brook trout, smelt
★ Boat ramp nearby
★ Lakeshore sites (on Lake Superior)
★ Walk to town
★ Lake Superior access
★ Store, restaurant, laundry, playground, gaming room, historical museum

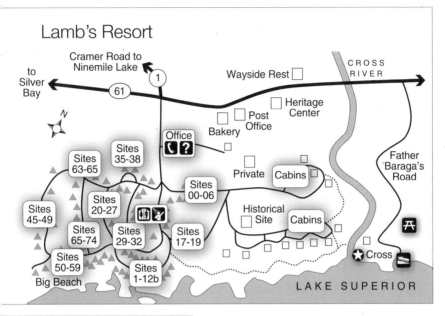

Lamb's Resort

CRAMER ROAD to Ninemile Lake
to Silver Bay
Wayside Rest
CROSS RIVER
61
1
Heritage Center
Post Office
Bakery
N
Office
Sites 35-38
Private
Cabins
Father Baraga's Road
Sites 63-65
Sites 00-06
Sites 45-49
Sites 20-27
Historical Site
Cabins
Sites 65-74
Sites 29-32
Sites 17-19
Sites 50-59
Sites 1-12b
Cross
Big Beach
LAKE SUPERIOR

GETTING THERE
Right off Highway 61 at Milepost 78.9 in downtown Schroeder.

From the resort, you can hike up the dramatic Cross River on a 1.5 mile trail that connects with the Superior Hiking Trail. Or you can wander over to Baraga's Cross and learn about the missionary's amazing crossing of Lake Superior. The Cross River Heritage Center has changing displays about local history and a gallery-like gift shop.

Sites #51 and 52 have their own private beach.

Tour historic Schroeder, Minnesota

 Schroeder Township is named after John Schroeder, a minor 19th century lumber baron who created an elaborate system to get white pines out of this rugged country. But the history of this region goes back even further. Be sure to visit **Father Baraga's Cross**, at the mouth of the Cross River across from the campground. Walk back up to the highway, across the bridge with great views of the waterfall, and down Baraga Cross Road to this large monument. It honors what some people call a miracle, where Father Baraga, "the snowshoe priest," landed in 1846 after crossing the open waters of Lake Superior in a small boat to minister to the Indians.

On your way to Baraga's Cross, stop in at the **Cross River Heritage Center**. This building was once the local grocery store and an early inn. Now there are exhibits about local history, and local crafts are available for sale.

On the way back, stop at the **Schroeder Baking Company**. Yes, there are yummy baked goods, plus hot coffee. But they also make a nice pizza and will deliver to your campsite. Now that's camping!

Visit Sugarloaf Cove

 A short drive back down Highway 61 will get you to **Sugarloaf Cove**, on the lakeshore at Milepost 73.3. Sugarloaf Cove is a great spot to rest and explore for a few hours. There's a one-mile interpretive trail.

Pick up the detailed booklet at the parking lot and head out; you'll learn about the history of log rafting on the site, the world-class examples of Precambrian lava flows, and the native forest restoration work evident throughout.

If you don't feel like hiking, take the short stroll from the parking lot down to the interpretive center, a beautiful log building with exhibits and a small reading area. A bit farther on is a large cobblestone beach, a terrific place to hang out, throw rocks and enjoy a small stretch of undeveloped Lake Superior shoreline. Be sure to check out the historic pictures of what the Cove looked like when it was a log rafting site for Consolidated Paper.

Sugarloaf Cove looks and feels like another state park, but it's actually owned and management by a nonprofit association. The middle of the site is a state scientific and natural area, protected because of the unique geology and rare plants. You might be tempted to take a beach rock as a North Shore souvenir, but don't do it. Everything here is to be left undisturbed.

Well-rounded cobblestones at Sugarloaf Cove invite exploration and playtime.

STATE PARK CAMPING

State park campgrounds fill up every night from mid-June to Labor Day. During the summer months, you'll need to plan ahead or be very flexible to get a site.

- If at all possible, make advance reservations at www.stayatmnparks.com. Reservations can be made up to 90 days in advance, so if you want to camp on a weekend in July, get ready for action in early April.

- Even if your camping trip is last-minute, you can try to make a reservation. You can make a reservation up until midnight on the day before your arrival. So if you're headed up the shore to camp on Friday, check the website Thursday afternoon and you might get lucky.

- If you don't have reservations, try to be at the park office by 9:00 a.m. or earlier, to get on the waiting list. At 11:00 a.m., the first people on the waiting list get the first campsite that has opened up. Your site might not be clear until 4:00 p.m., so be prepared to explore and wait.

- Check-out time is 4:00 p.m. If you're planning to stay another night but haven't paid for it, you need to pay and reregister by 11:00 a.m.

- Officially, only six people, one vehicle, and one tent are allowed per site. But park managers will work with you on this when you check in. Camping is limited to 14 days at one site.

- Sites that haven't been reserved are available first-come, first-served, just like the sites that don't require reservations. Check at the park office when you arrive to find out what might be available. Your site might be reserved by someone else the following night, so plan accordingly.

- State park campground reservations are site-specific. The site descriptions on the website are vague. For the most part, all of the state park sites are "good" sites. These listings point out the general qualities of different parts of the campground. Specific campsites are only good or bad depending on what *you* like.

Temperance River
State Park Schroeder, Minnesota

The upper campground at Temperance is RV-friendly, with great access to beaches, trails and the beautiful Temperance River gorge.

ONE STATE PARK, TWO GREAT CAMPGROUNDS. You've got options for North Shore camping at this state park. The park has great hiking and beautiful lakeshore, plus it's close to both Schroeder and Tofte with their museums, bakeries and stores. You can have a quiet place by the lake and still enjoy a wide range of activities here. The DNR's *Minnesota Conservation Volunteer* magazine named this one of the top four state parks for fishing, especially for trout and salmon.

The Lower Campground, on the west side of the river, is a traditional rustic campground, with vault toilets and water from a hillside spring. The access to the lake is superb here, with popular sites #40-44 looking right out on the beach and lake. Two cart-in sites are set off from the others, #46 and 47, and have direct access to the shoreline. These would be great for a larger family group.

The Upper Campground, on the east side of the Temperance River, is more luxurious and more typical of other North Shore state parks. That's where the shower house with flush toilets is located. There are even electric sites for RVs. Lake access isn't as good from the Upper Campground. But sites #3-6 above the Temperance River are especially attractive. In Loop B, #14 and 15 are the better sites, right on a trail to the shore. On Loop C, site #22 is the nicest, but #23, 25, 26, 28 and 30 are also fine, with privacy and a lake view through the trees. All campers can use the shower house, so if you're camped at the lower campground, you just have to walk or drive to take a shower.

Three cart-in sites are available in the Upper Campground, sites #31-33. There's lots of highway noise at these sites, and there's no direct access to the lakeshore.

OPERATED BY
Minnesota State Parks

OPEN
Year-round, but limited facilities October to May.

SITES
56, including 18 with electric hookups. Vehicle length limit 50 ft.

GETTING A SITE
41 sites are reservable; 15 are first-come, first-served. Reservations recommended.

RESERVATIONS
Visit www.stayatmnparks.com or call (866) 85PARKS.

FACILITIES
Flush and vault toilets, drinking water, showers. Lower campground water from artesian spring.

FEES
$18 non-electric, $22 electric

CONTACT
Temperance River State Park, Box 33, Schroeder, MN 55613 (218) 663-7476 www.dnr.state.mn.us/state_parks/temperance_river

You'll enjoy these activities & features

★ Canoeing
★ Swimming
★ Hiking
★ Fishing: brook trout, salmon
★ Lakeshore sites (on Lake Superior)
★ Lake Superior access
★ State park store with firewood & phone

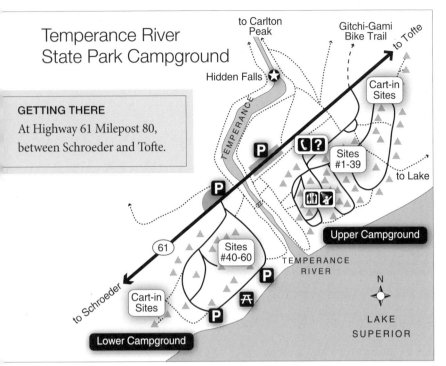

Temperance River State Park Campground

to Carlton Peak

Gitchi-Gami Bike Trail

to Tofte

Hidden Falls

TEMPERANCE

GETTING THERE
At Highway 61 Milepost 80, between Schroeder and Tofte.

Cart-in Sites

Sites #1-39

to Lake

61

Sites #40-60

TEMPERANCE RIVER

Upper Campground

N

to Schroeder

Cart-in Sites

LAKE SUPERIOR

Lower Campground

The lower campground at Temperance has a beautiful cobblestone beach right off the campsites, a perfect place to spend the day.

From the campground, it's a challenging 3.4 mile hike to the summit of Carlton Peak. Stretches of the Gitchi-Gami Trail run west to Schroeder and east to Lutsen.

Like most state park campgrounds, this fills up every night in the summer. See Best Camping Tips for state parks, on page 61.

Climb Carlton Peak

While Eagle Mountain gets the glory as the highest point in Minnesota, Carlton Peak is arguably the Gopher State's tallest mountain. Only 1,526 feet in elevation to Eagle Mountain's 2,301 feet, Carlton Peak is still nearly 1,000 feet higher than Lake Superior (just 1.3 miles away), and rises dramatically from the terrain all around it. It's a challenging hike perfect for the active family camped at Temperance.

The **Superior Hiking Trail** leads right from the riverside parking lot off the highway on the east side of the river. The trail is a bit confusing at first as it winds past the river's steep, deep kettles and canyons. Eventually the terrain flattens out, and after one mile the trail leaves the river and begins to climb. After three miles, the trail skirts the bottom of the peak, then reaches a spur trail to the summit. The summit is a dramatic rocky knob and provides rewarding views up and down the North Shore. This is a fabulous viewpoint for a trail lunch.

Carlton Peak was named after Reuben B. Carlton, who climbed the peak in 1848 with Colonel Charles Whittlesey. You're probably not thinking about sticky yellow notes up here, but this land was owned by 3M and only transferred to the state of Minnesota in the 1990s.

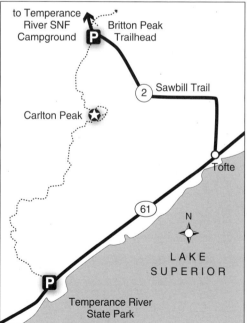

FOR MORE INFORMATION on the Superior Hiking Trail, see page 33, visit www.shta. org or call (218) 834-2700.

Temperance River
National Forest Tofte, Minnesota

Follow the beautiful Temperance River upstream from Highway 61
and you'll find this quiet and scenic National Forest campground.

WHILE THE NAMES ARE NEARLY THE SAME, this campground is
very different from the campground at Temperance River State Park.
This is a classic national forest campground, with quiet tent sites set
in the woods around a gravel road.

Just a short drive from the North Shore, here you can enjoy
rustic, quiet camping along a gurgling river. Nine private sites are
scattered through a spruce and birch forest. Sites #5 and 9 are closest
to the Temperance River, but all the sites have their own river
access trails.

While this is a nice quiet place to hang out by the river, it's also a good base for exploring the North Shore. It's just 11 miles to downtown Tofte and shorter drives to trailheads and put-ins. On your way to the campground, stop at the Forest Service Ranger Station in Tofte, ask about current conditions and collect maps for the area.

Carlton Peak is a great day hike destination, with some of the best views on the North Shore (see page 65). The Superior Hiking Trail trailhead at Britton Peak is the start of the trail up the east side of Carlton Peak, about nine miles back toward Highway 61. This access is shorter and easier than the more popular trail from Temperance River State Park.

Campers here should bring their mountain bikes: a network of dirt roads in the Superior National Forest beckons. The Honeymoon Trail (Forest Road 164) is a winding road through mature forest that heads east from the Sawbill Trail just 0.2 miles south of the campground. It's particularly scenic during fall, with lots of sugar maple turning gorgeous colors.

OPERATED BY
Superior National Forest

OPEN
Full services mid-May to September 30. Road not plowed in winter.

SITES
9

GETTING A SITE
First-come, first-served. Choose an open site, then register and pay at station near site #3.

RESERVATIONS
None

FACILITIES
Vault toilet, solar water pump.

FEES
$14

CONTACT
Tofte Ranger District
PO Box 2159, Tofte MN 55615
(218) 663-8060
www.fs.fed.us/r9/superior

You'll enjoy these activities & features

★ Fishing: brook trout
★ Riverside sites (on Temperance River)
★ Handicapped accessible toilet

GETTING THERE

From Highway 61 in Tofte, take County Road 2 (Sawbill Trail) 11.1 miles to campground entrance on left.

Sites #1-9

2

TEMPERANCE RIVER

N

to Tofte

Temperance River
National Forest Campground

Site #9 is set back from the campground road, with an easy trail down to the Temperance riverbank.

Ride the roads

Bike riding at a campground might make one think of little kids on their little bikes riding around the campground loops…around…and around again. But North Shore campgrounds are great bases for much more intense bike rides, and this Temperance River campground is close to some of the best rides.

Get one of the large fold-out Superior National Forest maps. Look for the winding roads. There's a lot of good riding out there.

Less than 300 yards back down the Sawbill Trail toward Tofte you'll find the **Honeymoon Trail** leading off to the east. Also known as Forest Road 164, this is a winding, narrow, gravel two-lane road through the heart of the North Shore maple forest. It leads about ten miles to the **Caribou Trail**, making a terrific round trip bike ride. "Road bikes"—bikes with skinny tires—might not work on this road, but any sort of "cross" bike or mountain bike will work great.

The Honeymoon Trail goes right by Honeymoon Mountain, about 2.5 miles in from the Sawbill Trail.

If you're ready for a more challenging bike ride, head just under a mile north on the Sawbill Trail to Forest Road 338. This is a narrower, rougher road that leads to **Pancore Lake**, Forest Road 339, and a counterclockwise 20-mile loop back to the Sawbill Trail.

FOR MORE INFORMATION on this last route and 10 other North Shore rides, read Steve Johnson's "Mountain Biking Minnesota" from Falcon Press. The Superior National Forest Visitor Map is available at all Forest Service ranger stations and by mail. Visit the Superior National Forest website for ordering info, or call (218) 626-4300.

Sawbill Lake Tofte, Minnesota

From this simple canoe landing at Sawbill Lake campground, you can head off into the BWCA for a day or a week. Although large, the quiet campground offers secluded sites.

CAMPING AT SAWBILL LAKE IS LIKE staying at a full-service wilderness retreat. At the end of a long day canoeing, stroll up to Sawbill Outfitters for a cold beverage or a hot shower. The campsites are spread out and private, under a canopy of older white pines, and many campers stay put for their whole vacation.

When pressed by a reporter, Sawbill Outfitters owner Bill Hansen said that site #5 is the most popular site of all. But all of the sites are good and most are quite spacious. For example, there would be plenty of room at any of the sites for a screen tent, which could come in handy on buggy June days. With all the activities and services available, and spacious sites, campers really settle in here.

Sites #9, 10, 12, 14, 17, 18, 20, 21, 23 and 25 are perched high above the lakeshore. The inner sites, numbers #29-40, are used less often and more private than the rest. To get to the lakeshore, all campers should use one of the two access trails that cut through the campground.

A canoe storage area is located by site #1. At the boat landing, there's a picnic area and a 500-ft. trail to the barrier-free fishing pier.

There are two or three perfect daylong BWCA canoe routes you can enjoy from the campground. You can head west for a loop through Sawbill, Alton and Kelso lakes. Or head north four miles on Sawbill to Ada Lake. Finally, you could head east to Smoke, Burnt and Flame lakes.

Sawbill Outfitters has a very respectable little store, where you can pick up almost anything you need, from food and beverages to a new sleeping bag. Hot showers are also available. The Hansen family is very involved in the North Shore community, so you might even pick up some local lore at the store.

OPERATED BY
Superior National Forest

OPEN
Full services mid-May to September 30.

SITES
50

GETTING A SITE
First-come, first-served. Choose an open site, then register at Sawbill Outfitters.

RESERVATIONS
None

FACILITIES
Vault toilets, solar water pump, dump station.

FEES
$14

CONTACT
Tofte Ranger District
PO Box 2159, Tofte MN 55615
(218) 663-8060
www.fs.fed.us/r9/superior

You'll enjoy these activities & features

★ Canoeing
★ Fishing: walleye and smallmouth bass
★ Fishing pier
★ Lakeshore sites (above Sawbill Lake)
★ BWCA access
★ Weekly interpretive program
★ Pay phone, firewood, showers, light groceries, light supplies, and canoe rentals at outfitters
★ Handicapped accessible fishing pier

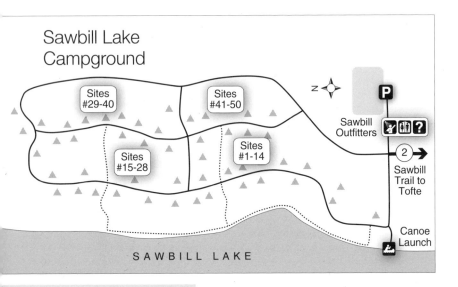

Sawbill Lake
Campground

Sites
#29-40

Sites
#41-50

Sites
#15-28

Sites
#1-14

Sawbill
Outfitters

P

2 →

Sawbill
Trail to
Tofte

Canoe
Launch

S A W B I L L   L A K E

GETTING THERE
From Milepost 83.4 on Highway 61, take County Road 2 (Sawbill Trail) 23 miles to Sawbill Lake.

Site #5 (above) is a favorite for many Sawbill campers. Designated trails (right) bring you from any site down to the lakeshore.

Sawbill Lake

Day paddle the BWCA with an outfitter

Here you are, camped beside a beautiful lake—and on the edge of a wilderness that encompasses over 750,000 acres of lakes, hills and streams. It's the Boundary Waters Canoe Area (BWCA). The "C" in BWCA stands for canoe—the only boat you can use on this lake. You might not have a canoe or maybe you've never been in a canoe before. You came to the right place.

At Sawbill Lake campground, you can rent a canoe for the day and take off to explore this unique area. It is one of only two campgrounds detailed in this book with canoe rentals right on site (the other is Trail's End campground at the end of the Gunflint Trail, page 106).

To enter the BWCA for a day trip, you'll need to get a day permit. At **Sawbill Lake**, and at most of the common entry points, there's a self-registration box near the put-in. Leaders of day parties have to know and abide by BWCA rules. Most important for day trippers are the rules about maximum group size (9), maximum number of boats (4), and restrictions on food packaging: no glass or metal containers.

Your day trip will start on Sawbill Lake. Sawbill is almost five miles long and full of islands. Register for a day-use permit at the boat

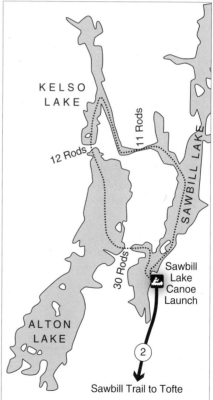

landing, and you can spend a full day just paddling around Sawbill. But the real Boundary Waters experience also includes portaging, so take the short portage into **Alton Lake**.

To make a day of it for beginners, do the six-hour loop from the north end of Alton into **Kelso**, then back to Sawbill.

If you can't tell a paddle from a puddle, hire a guide from Sawbill Canoe Outfitters to take you out for the day. A family of four can

go out for the day for about $200, all equipment provided.

If you're staying in another campground nearby, you can rent a canoe from an outfitter for a few days and use it at your campground. **Sawtooth Outfitters** on Highway 61 in Tofte is right on the way to most campgrounds, and they rent a variety of canoes. In Grand Marais, you'll find a few other canoe rental places as well.

FOR MORE INFORMATION, contact Sawbill Canoe Outfitters. Reach them by phone: (218) 663-7150; by e-mail: info@sawbill.com; or by mail: Box 2129, Tofte MN 55615. Visit them online at www.sawbill.com. Fisher Map F-5 covers most of these day trips. Sawbill Outfitters has its own custom map for sale at the store.

SUPERIOR NATIONAL FOREST "FEE CAMPGROUND" CAMPING

- Reservations are available for some North Shore Superior National Forest campgrounds (at www.recreation.gov). If you know you'll arrive late in the day, or if there's a specific site you really love, make a reservation.

- Most of the Superior National Forest campgrounds in this book are first-come, first-served. Try to arrive before lunch time and you'll have your pick of the open sites. Or to give yourself a good range of options, arrive Wednesday or Thursday, before the weekend crowds arrive.

- To choose a campsite, drive the loop or loops first; then find a campsite you like, and claim it by placing a folding chair, duffel or friend right in the middle of the campsite "driveway." Then go register, typically at the registration station. Be sure you have either a variety of bills or a checkbook and pen to pay.

- You might find that the only open campsites are away from the lake or river. All is not lost. Your campsite will feel like your own country estate by morning.

- If you really want one of those nice lakeshore sites that are full every night, you can casually check to see when that party is leaving by reading the dates on their permit…or you could just ask. Maybe you can move your camp the next day.

- Bring a big water jug. Most of these campgrounds now have just one drinking water supply, a solar-powered pump. Chances are good the pump will be a long walk from your campsite. It's nice to fill up once or twice a day rather than run back and forth all the time.

Baker Lake Tofte, Minnesota

Literally on the edge of the BWCA wilderness, the Baker Lake campground is remote and quiet. This boat landing is a short stroll from the campsites.

BEAUTIFUL TALL PINES GRACE THIS quiet secluded campground with direct access to a quiet chain of BWCA lakes. Even the outhouse, located at the base of more tall pines, is scenic. Generally, Superior National Forest rustic campgrounds have no drinking water, but this one is the exception, with drinking water available at a hand pump.

The author hesitated to put this campground in the book. It's so pretty and quiet...and free. Many of the national forest rustic campgrounds are a little overused. They might have strong fish smells in the campsites or garbage in the fire pits. This one is special. If you go, be sure to practice low-impact camping and leave your site cleaner than you found it. No garbage service is provided, so pack out everything you bring in.

Sites #1 and 2 are the best, with a trail leading to the canoe landing. But sites #3 and 4 are beautiful too, under stately white pine trees. You can bushwhack down to the water's edge from #3 and 4. Site #5 is not quite as nice but is even more private, as it is located all by itself off a side road just before the main fork in the entrance road. Site #5 has access to Horn Creek flowing from Baker Lake.

The campground is perched on a hill connected by footpath to the canoe landing for Baker Lake (see picture below right). If you want to cool off, the canoe landing is a decent place to jump in the water. The BWCA boundary is at the water's edge, so you can literally swim into the wilderness.

Get your free BWCA day permit at the canoe landing, and head across tiny Baker Lake for a 10-rod portage into Peterson Lake.

OPERATED BY
Superior National Forest

OPEN
Year-round, but road is not plowed in winter.

SITES
5

GETTING A SITE
First-come, first-served.

RESERVATIONS
None

FACILITIES
Vault toilet, hand water pump.

FEES
Free

CONTACT
Tofte Ranger District
PO Box 2159, Tofte MN 55615
(218) 663-8060
www.fs.fed.us/r9/superior

You'll enjoy these activities & features

★ Canoeing
★ Fishing: walleye, northern pike, perch
★ BWCA access

Baker Lake Campground

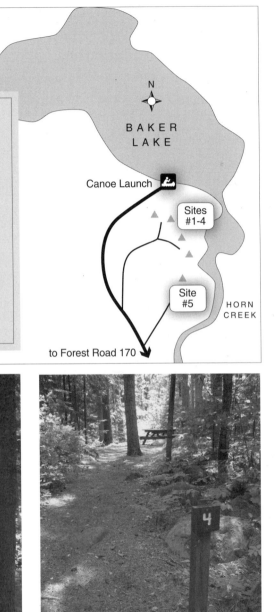

GETTING THERE

Take the Sawbill Trail (County Road 2) 17 miles to Forest Road 170 (The Grade). Turn right on Forest Road 170 and drive for 4.9 miles to Forest Road 1272 on left, with a sign for "Baker Lake Campground." Drive 0.4 miles to fork, take right-hand fork to campground. Left fork goes to canoe landing.

N

BAKER LAKE

Canoe Launch

Sites #1-4

Site #5

HORN CREEK

to Forest Road 170

Baker Lake might have the North Shore's most pleasant campground outhouse setting. Sites #3 and 4 (right) are tucked away in the pines.

Day paddle the BWCA on your own

Want to get a taste of the Boundary Waters but not ready to leave the comforts of car camping behind? Baker Lake is a great place to get the best of both worlds.

If you have your own canoe, bring it here. There's a day trip out of Baker Lake you're sure to enjoy. It's perfect for families and first-time wilderness paddlers. Canoeing with a family (especially with young children) requires patience, flexibility, and a willingness to embrace the journey rather than the destination.

The three lakes you'll reach on this easy adventure are small. That's good for your family, because small lakes are much less likely to get windy and wavy. Another good feature for families and beginners is that the portages are short. The first one, from Baker into **Peterson Lake**, is just 10 rods (160 feet). The second, from Peterson into **Kelly Lake** is just 3 rods (50 feet). In high water, you might be able to paddle right through to Kelly and skip the short portage.

Although Peterson and Kelly lakes are surrounded by steep hills, the lakes themselves are rather shallow and weedy. If you have non-paddling "duffers," assign one to watch for moose.

The campsites on Kelly Lake make for a pleasant family destination. Though you won't be camping, you can still use the BWCA campsites midday for picnics, swimming, and toilets. BWCA campsites generally offer a good canoe landing and a nice spot to eat. If a group comes along looking for a campsite while you're picnicking, good BWCA etiquette requires you to offer to leave and make way for overnight campers.

At the end of a great wilderness family adventure, you can return to your cot or your RV under the pines, relax and reflect on a great day in the Boundary Waters.

FOR MORE INFORMATION, check in at the Tofte Ranger Station.

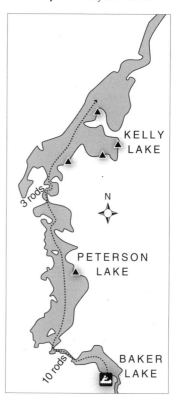

Crescent Lake Tofte, Minnesota

Paddling Crescent Lake is a popular activity for campers staying in the secluded sites of this quiet campground.

CRESCENT LAKE IS UNLIKE ANY OTHER CAMPGROUND on the North Shore. The sites are spread well apart along nearly one mile of shoreline. Do you like drive-up, lakeshore camping? How about walk-in, BWCA-like camping? Maybe you have a big rig you'd like to park under the trees. Or just maybe you're looking for some privacy and quiet. You'll find what you're looking for here.

The first set of campsites are reached with a left turn off the entrance road. You can car camp right along the lakeshore in sites #6-9. Site #9 is set aside for wheelchair users. These sites aren't very private, but they are convenient and scenic. Sites #1-5 are like remote BWCA sites, with a short hike in of 50-150 yards.

Sites #10-27 are much more spread out, in a forest of older pine, birch and spruce. Each campsite is a few steps up or down from the road, and they are visually separate from the road. This requires a short haul of your gear but provides great privacy. There is rough access to the lakeshore from the sites on the lake side of the road. Site #17 has its own long winding trail working down to the lakeshore, where you could stash a canoe. Site #26 is right on the water.

The last six sites, #28-33 in the loop, feel like a typical forest service campground and attract the RV crowd. Site #33 is usually occupied by the campground host. A view of pretty little islands off the shore make these an attractive option.

If you like to fish, or just enjoy a scenic view, check out the handi-capped accessible fishing pier. It's next to site #9 but it's available to anyone. The boat landing is also a fun area to poke around. If you have a canoe or kayak, bring it along; Crescent Lake calls out for exploration.

The campground map shows a hiking trail near sites #12 and 23, around "Pete's Point." The trail might not be maintained, so use with caution.

OPERATED BY
Superior National Forest

OPEN
Water and services available mid-May to mid-October. Road not plowed in winter.

SITES
33, including 5 hike-in, plus 1 group site.

GETTING A SITE
First-come, first-served, though accessible site #9 may be reserved through Sawbill Outfitters. Choose an open site, then register and pay at the far end of the road, near site #31. It's a long walk to the registration station.

RESERVATIONS
None

FACILITIES
Vault toilets, solar water pump.

FEES
$14

CONTACT
Tofte Ranger District
PO Box 2159, Tofte MN 55615
(218) 663-8060
www.fs.fed.us/r9/superior

Crescent Lake Campground

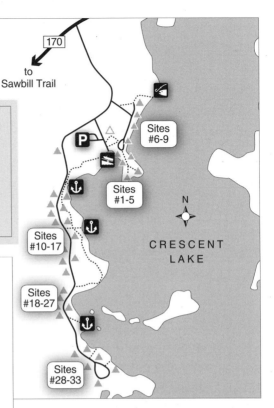

170

to
Sawbill Trail

P

Sites
#6-9

Sites
#1-5

N

Sites
#10-17

CRESCENT
LAKE

Sites
#18-27

Sites
#28-33

GETTING THERE

Take the Sawbill Trail (County Road 2) 16 miles, then turn right on Forest Road 170 (The Grade). Drive 6.8 miles to campground entrance on right.

You'll enjoy these activities & features

★ Canoeing

★ Fishing: muskie, northern pike, smallmouth bass, walleye

★ Fishing pier

★ Boat ramp

★ Lakeshore sites (on Crescent Lake)

★ Handicapped accessible (site #9)

Launch your boat at Crescent Lake's dock (above), or camp at the walk-in sites on the point (left).

Paddle big lakes

 At 700 acres in size, **Crescent Lake** is just big enough, with interesting little bays and islands, that you could have a great morning paddle poking around the lake in your canoe or kayak. If you have a lakeshore site, you can pull your watercraft right up to the shoreline. The walleye here are naturally reproducing and make for good fishing.

If you've explored Crescent Lake and still want more, you can work your way through a marsh at the north end of Crescent into pretty little Boulder Lake.

Paddle little lakes

 The Superior National Forest recommends a canoe route out of Crescent Lake: it's a chain of six tiny lakes off the south end of the lake. From Crescent Lake you enter Fleck, then Slip, Dogtrot, Bulge and Silver lakes. The route ends at Rice Lake, where you can leave a car off of Forest Road 340 on Forest Road

1856. The route is well-depicted on Fisher map F-6, "Brule and Pike Lakes." A cautionary note: the route may be marshy and has many portages, so plan accordingly.

Walk the campground

 It's a pleasant hike of nearly one mile just from one end of the campground to the other. Visit the campground host at the south end (site #31) or hang out at the fishing pier at the north end (by site #9). You can even make a loop of it with the rough trail connecting the boat launch and the Pete's Point trail.

Climb Eagle Mountain

See page 97 for a description of this hike, which is nearby.

Cascade River
State Park Lutsen, Minnesota

The Cascade River thunders through its gorge near the campground.

IF YOU LIKE TO HIKE, this is a great home base for your North Shore adventure. The Superior Hiking Trail runs practically right through the campground. You can hike the 7.7 mile Cascade River loop, summit Moose Mountain, or stroll along a rare undeveloped stretch of the North Shore itself.

The DNR's *Minnesota Conservation Volunteer* magazine named this one of the top four state parks for birdwatching, especially during fall hawk migration. They also named it one of the best for its scenic views.

The campsites are packed in a bit, without a lot of privacy from the campground road. If you're reserving ahead of time, you'll find sites

#A1, A2, A3, A4, A5 and B10 the best of the bunch. Most of the sites receive some road noise from Highway 61.

Be sure to walk down across Highway 61 and bring dinner down to the picnic area, where you'll find a great rocky shoreline and beautiful old cedar trees. At the peak of summer, kids enjoy splashing and even tubing in the Cascade River above the highway bridge.

If you're serious about hiking, try backpack camping "light." Cascade has five backpack camping sites, each with a three-sided shelter, pit toilet, picnic table and fire ring. One unique site is right on the shore of Lake Superior, about a one-mile hike from the campground. You can reserve these sites at www.stayatmnparks.com. You could even keep your heavy stuff at the car camping site and try an overnight off in the "wilderness."

In winter, camp here and explore the wide network of ski trails leading right out of your campsite. The "A" loop is open all winter. Reserve the heated picnic shelter and use it for an evening meal before returning to your cold tent.

If you need a break from camp cooking, be sure to visit the Cascade Lodge restaurant across the river.

OPERATED BY
Minnesota State Parks

OPEN
Year-round. Limited facilities in winter (only "A" loop open).

SITES
40, plus two group sites. Vehicle length limit 35 ft.

GETTING A SITE
25 sites are reservable, 15 are first-come, first-served. Reservations recommended. Check in at the office.

RESERVATIONS
Visit www.stayatmnparks.com or call (866) 85PARKS.

FACILITIES
Flush toilets, drinking water, and showers May-October, vault toilets year-round, dump station.

FEES
$18 plus state park permit.

CONTACT
Cascade River State Park
3481 West Highway 61
Lutsen, MN 55612
(218) 387-3053
www.dnr.state.mn.us/state_parks/cascade_river

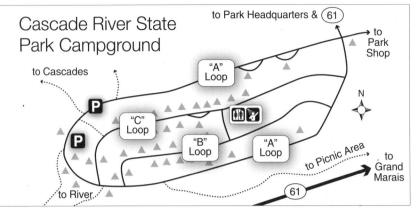

Cascade River State Park Campground

to Park Headquarters & (61)

to Park Shop

to Cascades

"A" Loop

N

"C" Loop

"B" Loop

"A" Loop

to Picnic Area

to Grand Marais

61

to River

GETTING THERE

At Milepost 100, turn inland at park entrance road. Campground is ¾ mile from highway.

You'll enjoy these activities & features

★ Canoeing

★ Fishing: brook trout

★ Hiking: 18 miles of trails

★ Lake Superior access

★ Restaurant, other services at adjacent Cascade Lodge. Firewood available at park office.

Roast marshmallows by the lakeshore in Cascade's unique picnic area (top photo), or float and play at the river's mouth (bottom).

Explore the shore

One of the best things about Cascade River State Park is the shoreline. The park includes a remarkable stretch of Lake Superior shoreline. There's so much shoreline, the park map doesn't even show it all.

Some of the park's best shoreline is right near the campground, in the picnic area. The picnic area is only for people with a state park permit on their vehicle. That keeps the crowds away. A trail to the picnic area leaves from the bottom of the campground's "A" loop.

At the picnic area, you'll find a beautiful forest of big, old cedar trees and a very accessible rocky shoreline. The picnic sites there are tragically under-used, but in great shape. The picnic sites have fire pits, making this one of the few places you can roast marshmallows right on the shore. If you're camping at Cascade, be sure to have at least one meal down on the lakeshore, or an evening of s'mores.

Thanks to the visionary founders of this park who acquired so much shoreline, you can take off up the shore toward Grand Marais. A hiking trail parallels the shoreline for almost a mile, reaching one of the park's backpack camping sites. For much of the way, you can scamper along the shoreline rocks.

Go climb a mountain

Cascade is definitely a hiker's park. There are three main destinations: Lookout Mountain, Moose Mountain, and the Cascade River Loop. **Lookout Mountain** is on the west side of the Cascade River and is a four-mile loop from the campground. The hike to **Moose Mountain** is a little easier, about 3.5 miles depending on which trails you take.

Perhaps the most popular day hike is along the Superior Hiking Trail up the **Cascade River** itself. This is an eight-mile loop with a range of challenging terrain. Hiking it clockwise lets you enjoy highlights like a spur to a "secret" waterfall while you still have energy. You actually gain more elevation on this trail than on either of the "mountain" trails.

The Cascade River hike and the Lookout Mountain hike are described in "50 Circuit Hikes." The Cascade River loop is featured in most North Shore hiking guides, including "50 Circuit Hikes," "Hiking Minnesota" and "Guide to the Superior Hiking Trail."

Grand Marais RV Park and Campground
Grand Marais, Minnesota

From the tenting area at Grand Marais RV Park and Campground, you can walk right out to a Lake Superior cobblestone beach.

THIS IS ABSOLUTELY FULL-SERVICE CAMPING in a terrific location. With 300 sites, you can find almost any kind of camping you like. There are three distinct camping areas: a dense RV park with long-term campers near the office and the marina (sites #1-102), an open field with some primitive tenting sites right off the beach (sites #101W-176W), and a forested tenting area with no services (sites #200-215). Then there's a large middle area that offers a little bit of everything (sites #1W-100W).

Tent campers will prefer sites #200-215, in a wooded area with easy access to the Honeymoon Bluff Trail, or the primitive waterfront sites #163W-176W adjacent to a beautiful cobblestone beach. These sites are in an open field but back up to some shoreline shrubbery.

Spend a rainy day at the indoor pool, hike the rugged 3⁄4 mile loop trail to Honeymoon Bluff, or hang out at the marina and swap fish stories…all right in the campground.

North House Folk School is right next door. Downtown Grand Marais is just four blocks away, full of restaurants and shopping, beaches and scenic Artists Point.

This isn't just a campground, it's a neighborhood. Many of the sites nearest the office are long-term rentals and outside these trailers are flower gardens and serious lawn furniture. "Residents" even pick up their mail at the office. Get to know the locals!

OPERATED BY
City of Grand Marais

OPEN
May 1 to late October

SITES
300 sites, 152 full hookups including sewer, 44 no hookups, 104 just water and electric. Also two group sites.

GETTING A SITE
Register at the office.

RESERVATIONS
Taken after January. Site-specific reservations may be possible. (218) 387-1712 or (800) 998-0959.

FACILITIES
Flush toilets, drinking water, showers, dump station.

FEES
$22-$36

CONTACT
Grand Marais Recreation Area, PO Box 820 Grand Marais, MN 55604 (218) 387-1712 www.grandmaraisRVParkand Campground.com

Campers relax on the shores of the Grand Marais harbor.

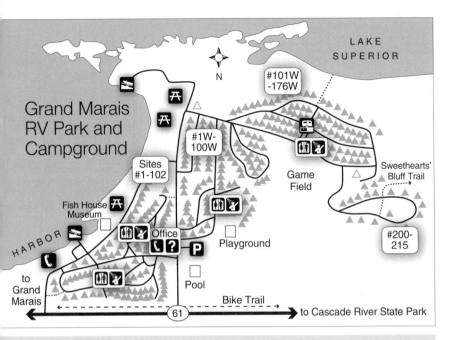

LAKE SUPERIOR

Grand Marais
RV Park and
Campground

#101W -176W

N

#1W- 100W

Sites #1-102

Game Field

Sweethearts' Bluff Trail

#200- 215

Fish House Museum

HARBOR

Office

Playground

P

to Grand Marais

Pool

Bike Trail

61

to Cascade River State Park

GETTING THERE
Campground is located on the western edge of Grand Marais.

You'll enjoy these activities & features

★ Hiking
★ Canoeing/kayaking
★ Swimming (in city pool)
★ Charter fishing on Lake Superior
★ Boat ramp
★ Lakeshore sites (on Lake Superior)
★ Lake Superior access
★ Walk to town
★ Pay phones, Wi-Fi, ice, supplies, playground, basketball hoop, horseshoes

This campground is right next to fun and busy Grand Marais.

Although the Grand Marais RV Park and Campground doesn't provide a wilderness experience, you can have a great family vacation based here. The campground is in town, with a short and scenic walk to anything, from a history museum to boutique shopping.

FOR MORE INFORMATION on all Grand Marais has to offer, go to www.grandmarais.com

Shop Grand Marais

Downtown Grand Marais is a compact cluster of shops and restaurants, located at the water's edge. Some stores come and go, but most have been around for years. Personal favorites include:

Joynes Ben Franklin: Narrow aisles lead through towering piles of woolen wear, work pants and practical shoes. Locals refer to the store as the "shoe museum," since they have footwear in stock from decades past. There's something for everyone, include practical camping supplies, cheap plastic toys, and souvenirs.

Sivertson's Gallery: The Sivertson family were long-time commercial fishers and have turned their eye to art. The gallery on Wisconsin Street features local artists (including Sivertson family members) and artists from the far north. There's also handcrafted jewelry, pottery and note cards.

The best selection of camping gear downtown is at the **Lake Superior Trading Post**. The two local bookstores—**Birchbark Books & Gifts** and **Drury Lane**—will supply your vacation reading.

Eat Grand Marais

Who needs to cook? Or dress up? Grand Marais dining ranges from casual fast food to, well, casual fine food.

Campers are looking for hearty meals they can't make on a propane stove. They might be looking to get out of

The Angry Trout, a nearby restaurant.

the rain, too. **Sven and Ole's** is a long-time family favorite for great pizza and its casual environment. But much closer to the campground you'll find the **Angry Trout,** a masterpiece of small-town cuisine featuring local organic dishes.

Gun Flint Tavern is popular with the micro-brew crowd. For hearty local fare, you might try one of the newer restaurants in town, the **Crooked Spoon** or, closer to the campground, the **Wild Onion Café.**

If you're still committed to campground cooking, you'll find great supplies at the **Cook County Whole Foods Co-op,** on the east side of downtown.

Learn at North House Folk School

The Grand Marais campground is ideally located for students at the North House Folk School. North House provides in-depth workshops on traditional crafts and skills. You can practice your rosemaling, build your own casket, or learn birds by their calls. The sailboat *Hjordis* takes short trips every day around the harbor and out to the open lake. The school is in a compact campus right on the waterfront, right next to the campground.

FOR MORE INFORMATION, visit www.northhouse.org.

Sail the *Hjordis* with North House Folk School

CAMPING THE NORTH SHORE? YOU WANT TO HAVE A BOAT!

Motorboat, canoe or kayak? If you can bring one of these, it will make your great North Shore camping experience even better.

Every campground in this book is on a body of water: a big lake, a little lake, or a river. Whatever its size, there's a watercraft for you. Please don't bring a "personal watercraft" to these campgrounds. These are quiet places and most campers don't want the noise or commotion of a Jet-Ski.

Motorboat. 92% of all boating by Minnesotans is in a motorboat. When camping in the North Shore area, the classic 15-foot motorboat is great for inland lakes. Most inland campgrounds on lakes have some sort of boat launch facility, so you can trailer your boat to the site and launch it there. Then, in a fun twist, you can pull it up at your campsite. **Two Island Lake, Crescent Lake, Indian Lake** and **Ninemile Lake** campgrounds are great for motorboats.

Canoe. An open canoe is perfect for almost all North Shore campgrounds. You can paddle around your lake and even go into the Boundary Waters Canoe Area. Particularly well-suited for canoes are **Eighteen Lake, Sawbill Lake, Baker Lake, Kimball Lake** and **Trail's End** campgrounds. You can rent a canoe at many outfitters, including Sawtooth Outfitters in Tofte.

Sea kayak. A sea kayak is great for adults and children 14 and older, especially on big Lake Superior. The low center of gravity and closed deck make it possible to be safe in the larger waves and stronger winds of Lake Superior. If you're staying at **Burlington Bay, Grand Marais Municipal, or Gooseberry Falls, Split Rock Lighthouse, or Temperance River State Parks,** you have easy access to kayak put-ins on Lake Superior. **Devil Track,** on Devil Track Lake, is also big and open and good for sea kayaks. Try Superior Coastal Sports in Grand Marais or Sawtooth Outfitters in Tofte for classes and rentals to introduce you to this great watercraft.

Devil Track Grand Marais, Minnesota

Situated on high ground with fabulous, open views, the private and secluded campsites here have direct access to pretty Devil Track Lake.

CLOSE ENOUGH TO TOWN, but with enough activity right here, you and the family could easily spend a week at this campground and not get bored. The sites with direct lake access are very pleasant and worth getting here early for. Each lakeshore site has views and access to the shore.

The sites tend to be very spacious and nicely secluded from each other. Long flat driveways accommodate big rigs. Sites #1-10 are secluded from the road as well, while the rest are a bit more public.

Devil Track is a big and busy lake, but is still nice for canoeing on calm days. Sites #14 and 15 have poor tent pads, so leave these for the RVs.

The Ojibwe name for this lake is "Manido bimadagakowini zibi," which has been translated as "The spirit's walking place on the ice river." That's probably a reference to the Devil Track river that empties from this lake into Lake Superior.

It's just five miles to the Eagle Mountain trailhead along Forest Service roads. So in your spare time, you can climb to the highest point in Minnesota.

OPERATED BY
Superior National Forest

OPEN
Full services mid-May to September 30. Road not plowed in winter.

SITES
16

GETTING A SITE
First-come, first-served. Choose an open site, then register and pay at station near site #1.

RESERVATIONS
None

FACILITIES
Vault toilet, solar water pump.

FEES
$15

CONTACT
Gunflint Ranger District
2020 W. Highway 61
Grand Marais, MN 55604
(218) 387-1750
www.fs.fed.us/r9/forests/
superior/contact/

You'll enjoy these activities & features

★ Canoeing
★ Fishing: walleye, smallmouth bass, northern pike
★ Boat access
★ Lakeshore sites (on Devil Track Lake)

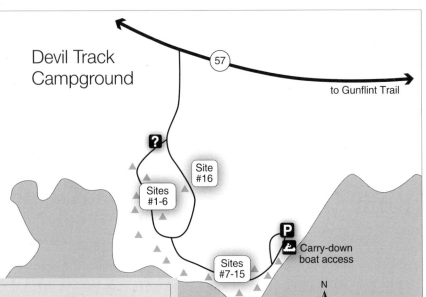

Devil Track Campground

57

to Gunflint Trail

Site #16

Sites #1-6

P

Carry-down boat access

Sites #7-15

N

DEVIL TRACK LAKE

GETTING THERE

Take the Gunflint Trail four miles and turn left on County Road 8 (Devil Track Road). Drive 5.6 miles past the general store and turn left on County Road 57 (still signed "Devil Track Road"). Drive 2.7 miles to campground sign and turn left on Forest Road 1612.

You'll feel much farther away from Grand Marais than just 12 miles at this scenic campground.

Climb Eagle Mountain

Climbing Eagle Mountain is a good patriotic experience for Minnesotans. The six-mile round trip hike itself is not necessarily all that dramatic or challenging, but reaching the highest point of our fine state is a tribute to Minnesota's diversity of landscape and people. There are more dramatic peaks and ridges along the North Shore. However, this is a "must-do" for the serious hiker and peak-bagger. The summit is 2,301 feet above sea level.

It's true that Minnesota is not known for lofty rugged peaks. But "highpointers" (people who try to reach the high point of every state) rave about Eagle Mountain for its rugged and beautiful terrain.

If you're planning to climb Eagle Mountain, stop at the Forest Service Ranger Station in Tofte or Grand Marais to check on current conditions. The Eagle Mountain trailhead is on Forest Road 170 (The Grade), about halfway between the campgrounds at Crescent Lake and Two Island Lake. Once you reach the trailhead, fill out a BWCA day permit.

Bring plenty of water, since there is only one water source along the way. You can stop at Whale Lake about two miles in for a break before the summit approach. The last stretch to the top involves about 500 feet of vertical ascent, following rock cairns.

See "Hiking Minnesota" by John Pukite for a detailed description of the Eagle Mountain trail.

Two Island Grand Marais, Minnesota

Two Island campground is great for campers with motorboats. Many sites have jetties where you can pull up your boat during the day.

THIS CAMPGROUND IS CLOSE TO the Devil Track Lake campground. Since the general location is the same, why choose this campground? Two Island Lake has much more of a wilderness feel than Devil Track's open, busy waters. The campground is more woodsy and remote, with older birch and spruce and some pines mixed in. If you brought your motorboat and the weather is clear, you can easily pull your boat up at many of these campsites.

If you like to canoe, try the five-mile, three-portage Twin Lakes Loop canoe route just northeast of the campground.

Three distinct loops offer a nice variety of camping terrain. Sites #1-11 are flat and open, with sites #8, 10 and 11 situated above the boat landing with its pleasant dock. With one of the campground's two solar water pumps located right by site #11, these sites are convenient and popular.

The loop with sites #12-24 is nice and piney, with sites up on stony ridges. Sites #19-24 all have foot trail access to the water's edge for some shore fishing or sunset watching. Sites #20 and 21 are the best on this loop.

The southern loop, sites #25-38, is quiet and remote. There is no drinking water on this loop. Some sites are carry-down, where you park on the road and bring your gear down steps. Sites #32 and 33 are especially nice, with a grove of cedars and easy access to the lake.

Tent campers be forewarned: all of the tent pads have a thick layer of gravel, so bring big stakes and a stake hammer.

OPERATED BY
Superior National Forest

OPEN
Services May to October. Road not plowed in winter.

SITES
36

GETTING A SITE
First-come, first-served. Choose an open site, then register and pay at station by entrance.

RESERVATIONS
None

FACILITIES
Vault toilet, solar water pump.

FEES
$15

CONTACT
Gunflint Ranger District
2020 W. Highway 61
PO Box 790
Grand Marais, MN 55604
(218) 387-1750
www.fs.fed.us/r9/forests/
superior/contact/

You'll enjoy these activities & features

★ Canoeing
★ Fishing: walleye, smallmouth bass
★ Boat ramp
★ Lakeshore sites (Two Island Lake)

Two Island Campground

TWO ISLAND LAKE

N

Sites #1-11

27

to 8

P

Sites #12-24

Sites #25-30

Sites #31-38

GETTING THERE

Take Gunflint Trail four miles from Grand Marais to County Road 8, aka Devil Track Road. After six miles on paved road, turn right on unpaved County Road 27. Take County Road 27 for 4.3 miles to entrance on left side of road.

Site #20 (above) overlooks the lake. At site #32, you'll find these interesting old cedar trees by the shore.

S'more to See+Do

Bring the runabout

Many of the lakeshore campsites here have small cobblestone jetties built at the water's edge. When the weather is calm, campers can launch their small boats with outboard motors at the boat launch and then pull them up at their campsite for easy access. Then boaters can head out on the lake at sunset to catch the view or a few smallmouth. Sites #32-34 are the best for this, and sites #23-24 provide a nice sheltered cove.

Paddle Twin Lakes Loop

There's a fun little canoe loop just a short drive from the Two Island Lake campground. The Twin Lakes Loop is a three-mile route through four smaller lakes, with medium-length portages between them. It's perfect for a day adventure. Or if you have your heart set on wilderness camping but couldn't get a BWCA permit, you can make this an overnight adventure, no permit required.

Taking the loop clockwise, start on **Pine Lake**, then portage alongside a creek into **Kemo Lake**. There are backcountry camp-sites on both lakes, perfect for a picnic lunch. Kemo is regularly stocked with lake trout. From Kemo it's a 30-rod portage into steep-sided little **Talus Lake** (stocked

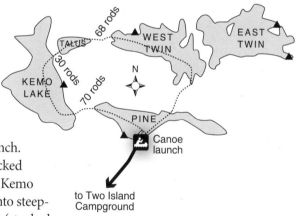

with rainbow trout), then a 68-rod portage into **West Twin Lake**.

To finish this loop, portage from West Twin near the boat landing back to Pine. Please respect private property here.

If you plan to paddle this route, stop at the Forest Service office in Grand Marais to ask about current conditions. Fisher map F-7 South Gunflint Trail and McKenzie map 100 cover this route completely.

Kimball Lake Grand Marais, Minnesota

Kimball Lake feel remote and quiet, even though you're only 12 miles from Grand Marais. Fish for trout or just enjoy the view.

KIMBALL LAKE IS A SMALL, QUIET LAKE. It's popular with trout anglers, who are not known to be terribly rowdy. The Kimball Lake campground is also small and quiet, with only 10 campsites, nicely spread out. Plus you get two lakes for the price of one here, with Mink Lake and its fishing pier and swim beach within walking distance.

The sites are pleasant and private, in a forest of older birch and fir. Sites #1-3 are on the road to the boat launch, so you might lose some privacy. If you get site #3, you can pull your motorboat up to your campsite. For more privacy, grab site #4, 5 or 6 on top of the hill and you've got just a short walk down a foot trail to the lakeshore.

Sites #5-10 on top of the hill are on a flat quarter-mile loop. The gravel loop calls out for kids to ride their bikes in endless circuits.

Kimball is popular among anglers for its stocked trout. If you don't have a boat, you can try your luck from shore.

The boat launch area on Kimball Lake is marginal for swimming. Mink Lake has more recreational facilities a short walk away, including a tiny roadside swimming beach 0.2 miles away from the campground, nice for one or two families to cool off. A barrier-free fishing pier is 0.3 miles away, down the shore from the swimming area.

Although it feels remote and quiet, Kimball Lake is actually the closest Superior National Forest campground to Grand Marais, so you can combine the quiet here with an easy trip to the bustling town.

Interesting fact: Kimball Lake feeds into Kimball Creek, which was named after Charles G. Kimball. He drowned in 1864 in Lake Superior at the river's mouth while participating in a state geological expedition.

OPERATED BY
Superior National Forest

OPEN
Full services mid-May to September 30. Road not plowed in winter.

SITES
10. Vehicle length limit 40 ft.

GETTING A SITE
First-come, first-served. Choose an open site, then register and pay at station near entrance.

RESERVATIONS
None

FACILITIES
Vault toilet, solar water pump.

FEES
$17 premium sites (#2, 3, 5, 6, 7, 8), $15 others

CONTACT
Gunflint Ranger District
2020 W. Highway 61
PO Box 790
Grand Marais, MN 55604
(218) 387-1750
www.fs.fed.us/r9/forests/superior/contact/

You'll enjoy these activities & features

★ Canoeing
★ Fishing: brown trout, rainbow trout, splake
★ Swimming (on Mink Lake)
★ Fishing pier (on Mink Lake)
★ Boat ramp

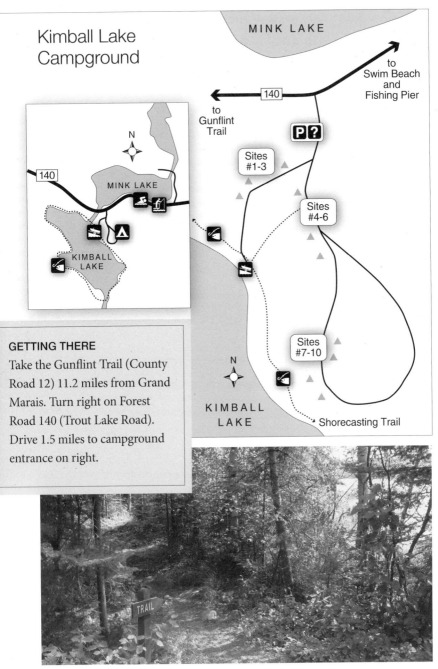

Kimball Lake
Campground

MINK LAKE

to
Swim Beach
and
Fishing Pier

140

to
Gunflint
Trail

P ?

Sites
#1-3

Sites
#4-6

N

140

MINK LAKE

KIMBALL
LAKE

Sites
#7-10

N

KIMBALL
LAKE

Shorecasting Trail

GETTING THERE
Take the Gunflint Trail (County Road 12) 11.2 miles from Grand Marais. Turn right on Forest Road 140 (Trout Lake Road). Drive 1.5 miles to campground entrance on right.

TRAIL

A rough trail, used by shore-casting trout anglers, circles Kimball Lake.

Shore cast for trout

Both Kimball Lake and its sister **Mink Lake** support healthy trout populations, stocked every year with rainbow trout.

Mink Lake has a barrier-free fishing pier; you can drive to a nearby parking lot—it's 100 feet to the pier. If you're staying at the Kimball Lake campground, you can get right to the water's edge at the boat launch. But for a classic trout-fishing adventure, try shore casting from the rough trail circling Kimball Lake.

The Minnesota DNR says that rainbow trout are most active in June and July, with the best fishing in the evenings when they're feeding on insects. If you're fly fishing, the DNR recommends using dry flies or nymphs. Shore casters, the DNR says, should use small crankbaits, spinners, or spoons.

The 1.8 mile trail around Kimball Lake isn't just for anglers, but don't expect great hiking. You'll be ducking under fallen branches and climbing over deadfalls.

If Kimball and Mink don't offer enough trout fishing for you, try the "real" **Trout Lake**. Keep heading east another mile or two on Forest

Road 140 to Trout Lake (turn left on Forest Road 308 to carry-down boat landing). There are natural lake trout here, plus stocked rainbow trout.

Finally, brook trout fans can hike into **Boys Lake**, just north of Mink Lake.

All these lakes require a trout stamp for anglers. Special seasons apply to brook-trout fishing; make sure you know the rules before heading out.

FOR MORE INFORMATION, see www.dnr.state.mn.us/fish/trout

Trail's End Grand Marais, Minnesota

Where the civilized Gunflint Trail runs into the wilderness canoe country, you'll find beautiful Trail's End campground and its lakeshore sites. This was the view from site #18 before the 2007 Ham Lake fire.

IT'S A LONG DRIVE FROM THE NORTH SHORE, but this campground is so special, it's worth it. Even after the Ham Lake Fire burned through here in May 2007, Trail's End still provides an amazing setting and offers a great base for wilderness adventures.

The campground covers an unusual peninsula, with Gull Lake on the north side, and the Seagull River plummeting from one wide pool to another on the south and west sides. The canoe portage around the rapids runs right through the campground.

The May 2007 fire left a dramatically changed environment, with some areas completely burned and others left untouched. Over the next 10 years, it will be fascinating to watch how the forest responds.

Sites #1-13 all offer water hook-ups for RVs, but are quite nice for tenting as well. The section with sites #3-13 is closed most summers until July to protect a nesting site for bald eagles.

Sites #15-17 are all walk-in sites, but it's only 30-40 yards in.

Sites #18 and 19 are up on a beautiful rocky knob overlooking the rapids. Sites #21 and 22 would be ideal for a large group to reserve at the same time, perched with their own outhouse and water supply high above a broad stretch of the Seagull River. The three sites at the other end are more closed in and have steep drop-offs.

OPERATED BY
Superior National Forest

OPEN
May to October

SITES
32, including 13 with water hook-ups. Vehicle length limit 20-40 ft.

GETTING A SITE
All sites can be reserved. Reservations recommended. Unreserved sites are available first-come, first-served. Check in with the campground host on arrival.

RESERVATIONS
Visit www.recreation.gov or call (877) 444-6777

FACILITIES
Vault toilets, drinking water.

FEES
$15-$20

CONTACT
Gunflint Ranger District
2020 W. Highway 61
Grand Marais, MN 55604
(218) 387-1750
www.fs.fed.us/r9/forests/superior/contact/

From the Trail's End campground you can paddle right up to gigantic Saganaga Lake and on to the fur trade canoe route known as the Voyageurs Highway.

Trail's End Campground

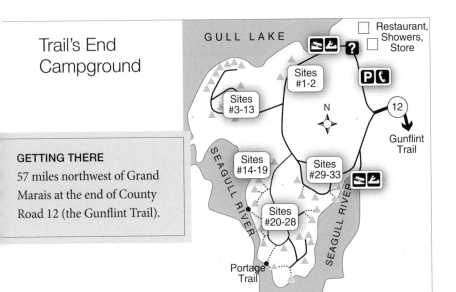

GULL LAKE

Restaurant, Showers, Store

Sites #1-2

Sites #3-13

N

12

Gunflint Trail

Sites #14-19

Sites #29-33

SEAGULL RIVER

Sites #20-28

SEAGULL RIVER

Portage Trail

GETTING THERE
57 miles northwest of Grand Marais at the end of County Road 12 (the Gunflint Trail).

You'll enjoy these activities & features

★ Canoeing
★ Fishing: walleye, whitefish, pike
★ Boat ramp
★ Lakeshore sites (on Gull Lake and Seagull River)
★ BWCA access
★ Store, shower, and restaurant at Way of the Wilderness resort.

A screen tent makes this Trail's End riverside campsite perfect.

Sites #27 and 28 are off by themselves down low near the water, and could also be reserved together for a group outing. You could pull your motorboat up on site #27.

Sites #29-33 are up on a ridge, with some significant rock exposure. Site #33 is a classic "billy goat" site, where you have to scramble up a bunch of granite to reach the site itself.

S'more to See+Do

Explore the changing landscape

This landscape has been seared by flames. In May 2007, a massive forest fire, the **Ham Lake Fire**, burned right through the Trail's End campground. This fire came just nine months after the **Cavity Lake Fire** burned through forest to the west. Here, you can get a feel for the power of these natural events to recreate the landscape.

Virtually any day trip you do from Trail's End campground will get you into more burned-over areas. The more time you spend in these areas, the more you can see how the fire burned. Did it burn whole trees, or did it sweep along the ground? Did it fry the soil down to bedrock, or just dust across the grasses? What happened to the trees that were knocked down in the 1999 July 4th windstorm?

Hikers interested in the effects of the fires will particularly enjoy the **Magnetic Rock Trail** (trailhead is 8 miles east of Trail's End campground, on the Gunflint Trail). The fire burned right across the trail, sometimes intensely, sometimes gently.

Everywhere you look or visit here has been burned by fire. Major fires in 1976 burned the area across the river from the campground, and at the Magnetic Rock Trail as well. Intentional fires were set on the edge of the blowdown area near the Gunflint Trail; these prescribed burn areas success-fully stopped the Cavity Lake Fire from spreading and damaging resorts and homes on the Gunflint.

The 2007 Ham Lake Fire burned the trailhead sign.

Judge C.R. Magney
State Park Hovland, Minnesota

Cross the Brule River bridge right out of the Judge C.R. Magney State Park campground and hike up to the Devil's Kettle.

IF YOU WANT TO EXPLORE THE TIP of the Minnesota Arrowhead, this is your best bet for a campground home base. There's two full days' worth of hiking here, plus it's the best tent camping for visitors to Grand Portage, the Arrowhead Trail and Isle Royale.

The campground is built on the site of an old Works Progress Administration camp, and you'll find remnants throughout, including cement foundations. Unfortunately, there is no direct access to the Lake Superior shore in the park.

The sites around the outside of the loop have the best privacy, including reservable sites #1, 5, 6, 8, 10, 11 and 12. The first-come, first-served sites are also more private. Site #1 is the top pick, with fewer neighbors and more daylight than the rest.

From the campground, you can hike to the mysterious Devil's Kettle, where half of the river disappears into a cave. Or head west or east on the Superior Hiking Trail.

For the naturalist, there's the Timberdoodle Trail, a new interpretive trail that starts by the campground. It circles for a mile past interpretive signs that help with plant identification.

The Grand Portage area, with its state park, national monument, and casino, is just 25 miles up the road and well worth a day trip.

The original 160 acres of this park was purchased for $5,000 in 1957. The park was first named Brule River State Park, but the name was changed in 1962 to honor Judge Clarence Reinhold Magney, probably the most important figure in the creation of North Shore state parks.

OPERATED BY
Minnesota State Parks

OPEN
May to October

SITES
27. Vehicle length limit 45 ft.

GETTING A SITE
17 sites can be reserved, 10 are first-come, first-served. Reservations recommended.

RESERVATIONS
Visit www.stayatmnparks.com or call (866) 85PARKS.

FACILITIES
Showers, drinking water, flush toilets, vault toilets.

FEES
$18, plus state park permit.

CONTACT
Judge C.R. Magney State Park
4051 E. Highway 61
Grand Marais, MN 55604
(218) 387-3039
www.dnr.state.mn.us/state_parks/judge_cr_magney

You'll enjoy these activities & features

★ Fishing: brook trout
★ Hiking
★ Restaurant across the highway

This park was originally called Brule River State Park when it first opened in 1957, but the name was soon changed to honor the great North Shore conservationist, Clarence R. Magney.

Judge C.R. Magney State Park Campground

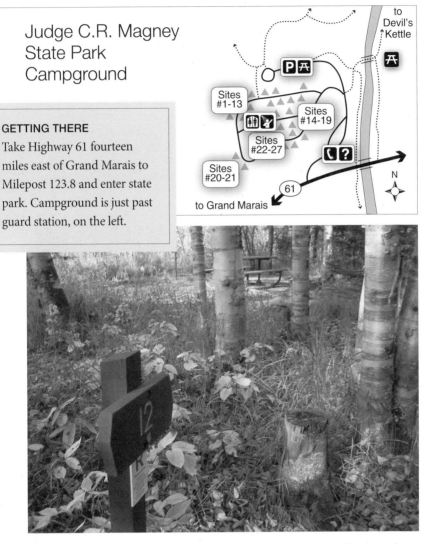

GETTING THERE

Take Highway 61 fourteen miles east of Grand Marais to Milepost 123.8 and enter state park. Campground is just past guard station, on the left.

Map labels:
to Devil's Kettle
Sites #1-13
Sites #14-19
Sites #22-27
Sites #20-21
61
to Grand Marais
N

There's not much privacy between Magney's sites—the sites are close together and the forest is thin. Reserve a site on the outside of the loop, such as #11 or #12 shown here, if you want more privacy.

Hike to the Devil's Kettle

For campers at Judge C.R. Magney State Park, this is a must-do hike. Not only is it a nice short hike along the Brule River, it takes you to the **Devil's Kettle**, a North Shore landmark and real-life mystery. The Brule River splits into two parts, but one part disappears into a cavern. No one has figured out where the disappearing water emerges. It's a one-mile walk to the falls, making a two-mile round trip. The hike is family-friendly, with a wide trail and many wooden steps with railings.

To reach the trail from the campground, return along the campground road and cross the entrance road. A footbridge takes you across the Brule River and into the picnic area. The trail is easy to find off to the left. You're actually on the Superior Hiking Trail here, so you'll see their distinctive trail signs as well.

The trail stays up on the river bluff for nearly the whole route, then descends down a long set of steps to the river and the Devil's Kettle. The steps have rest platforms with sturdy wooden benches; you may want to use these on the way up.

Serious hikers can continue on the trail another 5.5 miles to the next Superior Hiking Trail trailhead on Camp 20 Road.

Have tea with the Cree

For a special treat, dress up a bit, walk across the highway and visit the restaurant at **Naniboujou Lodge** with its incredible Cree-inspired dining room. Try the afternoon tea, served every day from 3–5 p.m.. As a customer, you can enjoy the Lodge's expansive cobblestone beach before or after dining.

Explore Grand Portage

Judge C.R. Magney State Park is a great base to explore the Grand Portage area. The attractions you'll find in Grand Portage are well worth the 20-mile drive from camp.

In Grand Portage, you'll find a national monument dedicated to fur trade history, a gorgeous waterfall, fascinating Ojibwe culture, and even a few good hikes. The new **Grand Portage National Monument**

visitor center opened in 2007, a great place to start your day.

To experience the national monument fully, set aside at least three hours. That gives you time to settle into the experience and understand the connections between natural resources and human activities. Be sure to talk with the costumed interpreters; they have a wealth of

knowledge about the fur trade and its place in North American history.

The annual **Rendezvous Days,** in mid-August, combines a powwow and a fur trade re-enactment; reserve your North Shore camp-site as early as possible for this event.

Grand Portage State Park is a few miles farther up Highway 61, up over the top of Mount Josephine. It's an easy stroll along a wide paved half-mile trail to the overlook of **Pigeon Falls.** The left side of the falls is the highest waterfall in Minnesota. The right side of the falls is actually in Ontario, Canada.

Grand Portage National Monument offers hours of family fun.

The other North Shore campgrounds:
43 more on the shore

THIS BOOK FEATURES the 23 best campgrounds on the North Shore. But other campgrounds exist on the North Shore—and most of them are pretty good. Here are the remaining campgrounds on the North Shore, from Duluth north to the Gunflint Trail.

Duluth area

▲ **INDIAN POINT.** With 70 sites spread around an open park-like area, this city-owned campground is located very conveniently on the bus line, next to the zoo and right on the scenic St. Louis River. Full hook-ups are available. Fish from the dock, hike the Western Waterfront Trail, bike the Munger Trail or just get to know your neighbors. For reservations call (800) 982-2453 or visit www.indianpointcampground.com.

▲ **FOND DU LAC CAMPGROUND.** This privately-owned campground is right on the St. Louis River, with 46 sites. There is little privacy but it's a great location if you like to fish, with a boat launch right in the campground and lots of shoreline dock for casting. Full hook-ups are available. No reservations. Call (218) 780-2319 or visit members.aol.com/vineslanding/a.htm.

▲ **BUFFALO HOUSE.** This is a RV-friendly campground popular with softball teams. It's right off Interstate 35 exit 245 and next to the Munger Trail. Call (218) 624-9901 or visit www.buffalohouseduluth.com.

▲ **SPIRIT MOUNTAIN.** Tucked into the maple woods above the ski area are 73 campsites, with electricity and water available. The sites appear to be too small and too hilly for most RVs. There are some cool hike-in tent sites, which can get buggy in the summer. You can hike on the cross-country ski trails or follow a spur trail down to the Superior Hiking Trail. Call (800) 642-6377 ext. 544, or reserve online at www.spiritmt.com

▲ **SNOWFLAKE NORDIC.** This popular Nordic ski center on the edge of town offers 25 quiet walk-in tent sites in summer. Some have electricity available, but the sites are for tents only. The chalet has showers, telephone, and firewood—plus the ski trails make for great hiking. Sites are $15 per night. Call (218) 726-1550 or visit www.skiduluth.com/Camping

Two Harbors area

▲ **PENMARALLTER CAMPSITE.** One of two remaining private campgrounds between Duluth and Two Harbors, this RV-friendly site is located between the expressway and the scenic highway. There are 24 campsites in an open field, some with full hook-ups. It's known for cleanliness and excellent customer service. Reservations accepted. Call (218) 834-4603.

▲ **KNIFE RIVER.** This private campground is a small, wooded facility with 30 sites, including tent sites near the Knife River. There's a rough trail leading to the river mouth on Lake Superior, where you'll find a beautiful cobblestone beach. A spur of the Superior Hiking Trail starts nearby, and the busy Knife River Marina is also within walking distance. Full hook-ups are available. Reservations available. Call (218) 834-5044 or visit www.kniferivercampground.com.

▲ **SULLIVAN LAKE.** This small DNR state forest campground is situated off the Superior National Forest Scenic Byway among tall pines. Eleven sites run up a hill beside the lake. A rough two-mile trail circles the lake. There is a boat launch (with fishing for northern pike), vault toilets, and a hand-pump for water. Site #4 might be the best tent site. The campground is managed by Split Rock Lighthouse State Park. Call the park (218) 226-6377 for more information.

▲ **SAND LAKE.** There's just one campsite at this Superior National Forest rustic campground right off Lake County Road 2, but it's free and scenic. Sand Lake is shallow and home to walleye, northern pike and bluegill.

Isabella area National Forest campgrounds

If you like the convenience of a developed national forest campground, three good ones are in the Isabella area. All are managed by the Tofte ranger district. If you plan to visit these, you might call ahead for current conditions. Call (218) 663-8060 or visit www.fs.fed.us/r9/forests/superior/ and look for "camping."

▲ **DIVIDE LAKE.** This fee campground is just east of Isabella and the Eighteen Lake campground along Forest Road 172. There are three sites here and a hand pump for water. Divide Lake is stocked for trout, and a hiking trail circles the lake. Divide Lake is so-named because it sits just on the south side of the continental divide separating the Lake Superior watershed from the Hudson Bay watershed.

▲ **MCDOUGAL LAKE.** This larger fee campground, with 21 sites next to a boat landing, has seen better days. There's a shallow, run-down swim beach and an overgrown nature trail. There are vault toilets and water comes from a solar-powered pump. Drive ten miles west of Isabella on State Highway 1. Reservations at www.recreation.gov.

▲ **LITTLE ISABELLA RIVER.** This pretty little fee campground in tall pines has 11 sites along a small creek, which is stocked with brook trout. Water comes from a hand pump. Most of the sites have access to the creek, but site #11 is the best of them. This campground is a great spot if you're looking for peace and quiet. It's 4.5 miles west of "downtown" Isabella on State Highway 1. Reservations can be made through www.recreation.gov.

Finland area

▲ **LAX LAKE RESORT AND CAMPGROUND.** Dotted among the cabins at this family resort are eight lakeshore campsites for RVs and tents. Lax Lake is just outside of Silver Bay on the Lax Lake Road. It's at the north side of Tettegouche State Park, so you can easily reach great hiking trails. Visit www.laxlakeresort.com or call (218) 353-7424.

▲ **WILDHURST LODGE.** This is a private campground just four miles north of Finland on Highway 1, with 17 sites, some along a small creek. A few have electricity for RVs. It's popular with ATV riders for its access to the Mooserun and Moosewalk state trails. Call (218) 353-7337 or visit www.wildhurstlodge.com.

Cramer Road

▲ **CROSBY MANITOU STATE PARK.** There's no car camping here, but pleasant, rustic sites are within a quarter-mile hike around scenic Benson Lake. This isn't cart-in camping like Split Rock Lighthouse State Park, but real hiking—and the Benson Lake sites make for an easy introduction to backpacking. Call Tettegouche State Park at (218) 226-6365.

▲ **HARRIET LAKE.** Past the Ninemile Lake campground, you'll find this Superior National Forest rustic campground. There are four sites and a boat landing near an open field, the site of a 1910 farm still maintained for wildlife. Anglers will find walleye and northerns in Harriet Lake.

▲ **HOGBACK LAKE.** Hogback is just west of County Road 7 along Forest Road 172. Hikers can enjoy a three-mile loop around Scarp Lake (see page 37). Hogback Lake is deep and clear, with an accessible pier for trout fishing. There are three sites in this Superior National Forest rustic campground, and pretty picnic areas for cooking dinner right on the beautiful lakeshore.

▲ **WINDY LAKE.** There's just one site at this Superior National Forest rustic campground. If you're a canoeist, you might stay here and paddle through Tee Lake to Silver Island Lake. Anglers find walleye.

▲ **KAWISHIWI LAKE.** Literally on the edge of the BWCA, this five-site rustic campground toward the end of County Road 7 on Forest Road 354 is spacious and open, with great access to day-trip canoe routes. The sites have lots of rock and pine trees. Up to nine parties a day enter the BWCA from here, so it's not the most private of campgrounds. But it's one of the best "free" sites.

West from the Cramer Road

▲ **SILVER ISLAND LAKE.** 2.4 miles west of the Cramer Road 7 on Forest Road 369, turn north on Forest Road 921 and drive 1.5 miles to this lake. There you'll find this Superior National Forest rustic campground. There are eight sites around a loop with a vault toilet in the middle. Two of the sites are right on the shores of Silver Island Lake. You can paddle and portage your canoe 60 rods into Tee Lake and 130 rods into Windy Lake.

▲ **SECTION 29 LAKE.** Head 1.5 miles north from Forest Road 369 on Forest Road 356. Watch for a signed road on left. There are four sites, including one right on the lakeshore with its own giant boulder. The Superior National Forest rustic campground is a bit scrubby, with a pit toilet out in the open, but good for canoeing and walleye fishing. There are ancient pictographs on Island River, off Comfort Lake, a few miles away.

East from the Cramer Road

▲ **WILSON LAKE.** 1.5 miles east of the Cramer Road, or 12 miles west of the Sawbill Trail, turn north on Forest Road 355, and drive one mile to the end. Wilson Lake is a pleasant Superior National Forest rustic campground with four campsites in a birch forest. The sites are above a good boat ramp with a dock for accessing the clear waters of Wilson Lake. Anglers find walleye and northern pike. You can also visit or fish in Little Wilson Lake, just west of the campground. The vault toilet is handicap accessible.

▲ **WHITEFISH LAKE.** 2.5 miles east of the Cramer Road on Forest Road 170, or about 11 miles west of the Sawbill Trail, turn north on Forest Road 348. Drive five miles to the end of 348, and you'll find three private campsites next to the lake lined with pine, spruce and boulders. It's a Superior National Forest rustic campground, with no services. There's also no boat ramp, just a carry down for canoes. You can access the near-wilderness Timber-Frear canoe route from here. Anglers find walleyes and northern pike, but no whitefish, in Whitefish Lake.

▲ **FOURMILE LAKE.** 5.5 miles west of the Sawbill Trail, look for the campground entrance on the south side of Forest Road 170. There are four sites in the campground, separated from the lake by a low and boggy area. The last site is the nicest. The boat landing has a turn-around for trailers. This is a Superior National Forest rustic campground.

▲ **TOOHEY LAKE.** Just east of Fourmile Lake (above), and less than five miles west of the Sawbill Trail, Toohey Lake is scenic but shallow. There are five sites in this free Superior National Forest rustic campground, three right near the mucky shoreline. The lake is ringed by distant hills, and the campsites are under big birch trees. There's a dock at the landing that reaches out to water one-foot deep at the end.

Sawbill and Caribou Trail area

Three more Superior National Forest "Rustic" campgrounds are found along the gravel roads between the Sawbill and Caribou trails.

▲ **POPLAR RIVER.** Along Forest Road 164 (Honeymoon Trail), five miles east of the Sawbill Trail and five miles west of the Caribou Trail, you'll find this Superior National Forest rustic campground. Four sites are scattered around an open brushy area along the upper reaches of the Poplar River, five miles west of the Caribou Trail and five miles east of the Sawbill Trail. It doesn't look like it's been maintained in years. Unless you're really committed to brook trout, there's not much to recommend here.

▲ **WHITE PINE LAKE.** Three miles west of the Caribou Trail on Forest Road 164, watch for a sign to this campground and lake access. Three sites are well spread apart in the woods near the boat landing. The last one has a partial view of the lake. There's a handicapped accessible fishing pier and the vault toilet is newer. The lake is big and has a few white pine. Anglers catch walleye and northern pike. Bring your mountain bikes for a fall color base camp from this Superior National Forest rustic campground.

▲ **CLARA LAKE.** Tucked way in off the beaten path on Forest Road 340, the three sites here are wooded and a long way (about 500 yards) from the lake and the primitive boat ramp. Not recommended.

Grand Marais area

▲ **GO-FER CABINS AND TRAILER COURT.** Yes, that is a campground right on the eastern edge of Grand Marais. Only ten sites, six with hook-ups. Call (218) 387-1252.

▲ **CASCADE RIVER.** This Superior National Forest rustic campground at the junction of Cook County Road 57 and Forest Road 158 doesn't have picnic tables at its four sites, but it's in a scenic valley with a brook trout stream cascading by.

▲ **EAST BEARSKIN LAKE.** This large Superior National Forest fee campground has 33 sites on multiple loops. Turn north (right) off the Gunflint Trail on Forest Road 146 and drive one mile to the campground entrance on the right. Even though it's right on a pretty lake, very few of the sites actually have lake access. Half of East Bearskin is in the BWCA, so there is quiet canoeing to be found here. Site #17 is the nicest, and sites #3 and 6 have pleasant views of Bearskin Lake. You can rent canoes or motorboats at Bearskin Lodge. A day-use area with a small beach is fine for hanging out by the lake.

▲ **FLOUR LAKE.** Access this Superior National forest fee campground by taking Cook County Road 66 off the Gunflint Trail. You can reserve one of the 37 campsites through www.recreation.gov. Like East Bearskin, these are pleasant sites but few have any direct access to pretty Flour Lake. The Honeymoon Bluff Trail makes for a nice 1.5 mile hike out of the campground, a quarter mile up the road, then up to a loop around an overlook. The campground is managed by Golden Eagle Lodge, a mile up the road or a half mile by lakeshore footpath. Visit www.flourlakecampground.com.

▲ **IRON LAKE.** Off the Old Gunflint Trail, this campground has only seven campsites. It was closed after the 2007 Ham Lake Fire and had not reopened when this book went to press. When it was open, reservations were taken at www.recreation.gov.

▲ **OKONTOE.** This is an interesting private campground along the shores of non-motorized Bow and Quiver lakes and can be found a half mile south of the Gunflint Trail on Bow Lake Road. The 32 pretty sites are scattered along the shore and in the woods. The campground offers a camp store, horse rides and worship services. Some electric hook-ups are available. There are flush toilets in the "outhouses." Sites #1-5 are right on a private little swim beach. Summer call (218) 388-2285. Winter call (218) 388-9423. Reservations available. Visit www.okontoe.com for more information.

Gunflint Trail resort camping

For a deluxe experience, try camping at a resort! You can put your tent up by a lake and eat in the lodge every night. These Gunflint Trail resorts offer camping:

▲ **GOLDEN EAGLE LODGE.** Nine sites, full hook-ups. Visit www.golden-eagle.com or call (800) 346-2203.

▲ **GUNFLINT PINES.** 26 sites right by Gunflint Lake, many with full hook-ups. Visit www.gunflintpines.com or call (218) 388-4454.

▲ **HUNGRY JACK LODGE.** On Hungry Jack Lake, secluded full-service sites. Visit www.hungryjacklodge.com or call (800) 338-1566.

▲ **NOR'WESTER LODGE.** Lakeside RV sites on Poplar Lake. Visit www.norwesterlodge.com or call (800)992-4386.

▲ **WINDIGO LODGE.** 10 campsites at this resort on Poplar Lake, with hook-ups. Visit www.windigolodge.com or call (800) 535-4320.

Grand Portage area

▲ **GRAND PORTAGE MARINA AND RV PARK.** Right behind the Grand Portage Lodge and Casino is an RV park with full hook-ups and a great view of scenic Grand Portage Bay. The small marina is popular with commercial fishermen headed to Isle Royale. Visit www.grandportage.com or call (218) 475-2476

▲ **GRAND PORTAGE STATE FOREST.** You'll need a good map to find these remote gems. The Grand Portage State Forest map is available at the Minnesota DNR office in Grand Marais or from Judge C.R. Magney State Park.

Head up the Arrowhead Trail (County Road 16) from Hovland to unique and rugged campsites on **ESTHER** and **DEVILFISH LAKES.** Winding dirt roads take you 5.5 miles off of the Arrowhead Trail, so these campsites are a long drive from Highway 61. Like the National Forest rustic campgrounds, these are free and small, with a few sites, a picnic table and an outhouse, but no water or garbage service. The five sites at Devilfish Lake are a little run-down. The three sites at Esther Lake are nicer, with a rocky point out on the lake.

At the end of the Arrowhead Trail, next to the **MCFARLAND LAKE** boat landing, are five more free campsites, providing direct access to two different BWCA entry points and the Border Route hiking trail.

These state forest campgrounds are managed by Judge C.R. Magney State Park. Call (218) 387-3039. Maps may be available online as well, through the Minnesota DNR.

RECOMMENDED READING

BEST
Camping
TIPS

- **50 Circuit Hikes: A Stride-by-Stride Guide to Northeastern Minnesota,** Howard Fenton (1999, University of Minnesota Press)

- **Boundary Waters Canoe Area: The Eastern Region,** Robert Beymer (2000, Wilderness Press)

- **Everyone's Country Estate: A History of Minnesota's State Parks,** Roy W. Meyer (1991, Minnesota Historical Society)

- **Fishing Lake Superior: A Complete Guide to Stream, Shoreline, and Open-Water Angling,** Shawn Perich (1995, Univeristy of Minnesota Press)

- **Guide to the Superior Hiking Trail,** Superior Hiking Trail Association (2007, Ridgeline Press)

- **Hiking Minnesota,** John Pukite (1998, Falcon Press)

- **Hiking Minnesota II,** Mary Jo Mosher and Kristine Mosher (2002, Falcon Press)

- **Rock Picker's Guide to Lake Superior's North Shore,** Mark Sparky Stensaas and Rick Kollath (2000, Kollath-Stensaas Publishing)

- **A Walking Guide to the Superior Hiking Trail,** Ron Morton and Judy Gibbs (2006, Rock Flower Press)

- **Waterfalls of Minnesota's North Shore,** Eve Wallinga and Gary Wallinga (2006, North Shore Press)

- **Wildflowers of the BWCA and the North Shore,** Mark Sparky Stensaas (2003, Kollath-Stensaas Publishing)

Group campsites

CAMPING WITH SCOUTS? Perhaps there's a family reunion in the making? Try a group camp for the ultimate bonding experience.

▲ **JAY COOKE STATE PARK (page 12).** Two groups sites are available, each about 150 yards from a parking area. Carts are available to haul your gear. There's a 25-person maximum, tents only. Reserve through www.stayatmnparks.com or call the park office directly.

▲ **INDIAN LAKE (page 20).** The group camp is in a large field off of Loop A. If site #25 isn't occupied, pay for that one too and your group can enjoy lakeshore access there. Reserve the group site through Split Rock Lighthouse State Park.

▲ **GOOSEBERRY FALLS STATE PARK (page 24).** The three group sites are accessed from a separate road off the main park road. The tent-only sites accommodate up to 50 people each. Each site has vault toilets. Drinking water is available near the shared parking area. You can use the carts to haul in camping gear. The Birch Ridge Camp contains two level camping areas. Pebble Creek Camp is the closest to Lake Superior and the Nestor Grade Camp has a large open grassy area and is handicapped accessible. Reserve a site through www.stayatmnparks.com or call the park directly. A trail leads one-third of a mile to the main campground shower house.

▲ **FINLAND (page 42).** Sites #25-29 are set off from the rest of the campground around an open field. Sites #27 and 28 are perched right on the Baptism River, so don't put the little kids there. These can be reserved all together for your group. Call the Tettegouche State Park office to make a reservation. The outhouse is a short walk through the woods by site #1 in the main campground loop.

▲ **TETTEGOUCHE STATE PARK (page 50).** Tettegouche has two primitive group campsites, each for up to 35 people. Parking is at the trailhead parking lot. Carts are available to carry your gear 150 yards in. Reserve a site through www.stayatmnparks.com or call the park directly for more information.

▲ **CRESCENT LAKE (page 80).** Tucked into the woods by the boat landing is a small group site. No reservations can be made, but contact the campground concessionaire, Sawbill Outfitters, for more information.

▲ **CASCADE RIVER STATE PARK (page 84).** The two group camps are far from the main campground, closer to the park office. They are for tents only, with a hike of about 75 yards to the campsites. Each site serves a maximum of 20. Water is about 300 yards away at the RV dump station. For reservations, visit www.stayatmnparks.com or contact the park office directly.

▲ **GRAND MARAIS RV PARK AND CAMPGROUND (page 88).** This extra-large campground has two group camp areas, one by the ball field and one near the boat ramp.

▲ **TRAIL'S END (page 106).** There's no official group campsite here, but with some creative reservations there's great group camping. The maximum for each site is nine people. Sites #21 and 22 are isolated from the others and have their own outhouse and water supply, so a group of 18 could use these; larger groups could reserve nearby sites #23-26 and a group of up to 50 could camp on this scenic dead-end campground spur.

Index

About There and Back Books

We live and play in northern Minnesota—a fabulous landscape filled with wild rivers, deep woods, diverse wildlife, and the greatest Lake. An abundance of terrific trails, campgrounds, state parks, outfitters, and lodging makes this landscape accessible to nearly everyone.

Still, many visitors (and natives) stay only on the beaten path. There's so much more to discover!

For every Gooseberry Falls State Park with its steady stream of gawking tourists, there are three beautiful unnamed waterfalls you can have all to yourself. For every Wi-Fi coffeehouse where you can sample "Moose Mocha" or "Sawtooth Sunrise," there are ten incredible rocky overlooks where you can sit and experience the real thing. And for every crowded campsite where you listen to your neighbor's radio until midnight, there's another campsite in the quiet woods on a quiet lake where all you hear are loons.

We want to help you find these wild places. It's amazing how good driving directions and a simple map can boost your confidence and get you "out there."

Our logo comes from a famous pictograph panel at Hegman Lake north of Ely, Minnesota, just inside the Boundary Waters Canoe Area Wilderness. With good directions and basic paddling skills, the average family could make a great day trip in to see them. And doesn't that guy look like he's embracing life and having fun?

We hope you, too, can look up in awe at this pictograph panel from a canoe. Guiding people to discover beautiful wild places—that's why There and Back Books was created.

We'll see you on the trail!

ABOUT THE AUTHOR

Andrew Slade's parents first set eyes on each other on the North Shore, and his life has centered there since birth—despite growing up in the Twin Cities. As a kid, he caught nets full of smelt at the Cross River, jumped cliffs into the deep pools of an unnamed North Shore river, helped to band woodcock in the open fields of North Shore homesteads, and shut his eyes tight each time the family wagon drove around Silver Cliff (note to today's drivers: don't worry, there's a tunnel through the cliff now and his eyes stay open). With his intrepid father, he had to abandon a mid-1970s assault on Carlton Peak due to a lack of recognizable trails.

As a canoe guide and outdoor educator in Ely, he learned that "sauna" is a three-syllable word (sow-ooh-nah). In his twenties, he bushwhacked by snowshoe much of what is now the Manitou-Caribou section of the Superior Hiking Trail. At age 28, in his "before kids" era, he was the editor and lead author of the first *Guide to the Superior Hiking Trail*.

Slade graduated from the University of Minnesota with a BA in environmental education and from the University of Montana with a MS in environmental studies. His favorite wildflower is *Mertensia paniculata*, the native North Shore bluebell.

Andrew has worked for environmental education and preservation organizations in Duluth and on the North Shore since 1992, including Great Lakes Aquarium and Sugarloaf. You can reach him at andrew@thereandbackbooks.com.

THERE AND BACK BOOKS
READ. GO. DISCOVER.

www.thereandbackbooks.com

Skiing the North Shore
A guide to cross country trails in Minnesota's spectacular Lake Superior region

By Andrew Slade $15.95

Get the skinny about the most gorgeous cross county ski trails in North America. Join Andrew Slade, an experienced guide and skier, as he takes you along all 700+ kilometers of trails that wind through the North Shore's city and state parks, a National Forest, and private ski areas. Here, perfectly groomed trails have earned names like Bear Chase, Otter Run, Mystery Mountain, Canyon Curves, and Lonely Lake.

This is a skier's ultimate guidebook to the North Shore—describing 35 groomed trail systems from Duluth-Superior to Grand Marais and the Gunflint Trail. You'll learn about hidden gems and rediscover well-known state parks. Slade offers useful information about challenging trails for the expert skier, gentle and fun trails for a family outing, scenic overlooks where you can stop for lunch alfresco, and lighted trails where you can enjoy a romantic night ski.

Written for all who love to ski—beginners, recreational skiers, families, experienced skiers, classical and skate skiers. Packed with useful information:

- **44 detailed trail maps** with driving directions to trailheads.
- **Helpful trails descriptions & difficulty ratings** to plan your outing.
- **Fees and pass requirements**…and free trails, too!
- **Resources for skiers,** including snow condition hotlines and web sites, equipment rentals, and road conditions.
- **Trailside lodging options,** from campsites to condos.
- **The author's top picks** for best trail grooming, wildlife viewing, most family-friendly, best views of Lake Superior, and more.

Published by There and Back Books. More info at www.thereandbackbooks.com